A GOD WHO ACTS

By the Same Author

The Christian Mind (Servant)
Where Do We Stand? (Servant)
The Secularist Heresy (Servant)

A God Who Acts

*Recognizing the Hand of God
in Suffering and Failure*

Harry Blamires

SERVANT BOOKS
Ann Arbor, Michigan

Originally published under the title *The Will and the Way*

Published by Servant Books, Box 8617, Ann Arbor,
Michigan 48107

Cover photo by Ed Cooper
Cover design by John B. Leidy

ISBN 0-89283-110-3
Printed in the United States of America

In place of a dedication, I should like to pay a public tribute here to the life and work of LEONARD CHALLIS, priest, a man of deep holiness, wisdom, and compassion, who spent himself, eventually to the exhaustion of physical and mental resources, in arduous and faithful ministry. This is the more appropriate because his desperate illness and tragic death, as well as his fervent teaching, have left their mark upon the following pages at many points. Yet, though it may help the reader to know that the need to come to terms with the spectacle of acute suffering underlies much that is said in this book, it would be wrong to dwell markedly on the dark evening of a life which was for the most part lived brightly in God's service. It is more proper to give thanks for all that God did through LEONARD CHALLIS during his long years of joyful and devoted ministry.

R. I. P.

Contents

INTRODUCTION
to the American Edition of 1981

A *God Who Acts,* first published in 1957 under the title *The Will and the Way,* is different in genre from those theological books of mine which Servant Publications has hitherto issued. Its concern is rather with personal spiritual life than with the public issue of sustaining doctrinal orthodoxy in the modern secular world. This does not mean that the book lacks close connection with my other works. The problems posed for the personal spiritual life which the book examines derive a special gravity from obstacles which the tide of secularism rolls under the believer's feet. *A God Who Acts* explores personal spiritual adjustments required of the Christian in a mental climate disturbed by the tensions and confusions analysed in my more directly polemical books like *The Christian Mind* and *The Secularist Heresy.* But, in so doing, it uncovers the truth that though men and women like to talk about intellectual obstacles to faith, in fact it is more likely to be sheer selfish appetite and wilfulness that stand in the way of Christian commitment.

In looking back to the first publication of *The Secularist Heresy* it was natural for me to try to place the book by reference to the changing relationship between the theological world and the world of secularised thought. By contrast, introducing a re-issue of *A God Who Acts* seems to call for reference to more private matters. For the book reads more like the record of a personal struggle than a document of public controversy. It seems preoccupied with the need to come to terms with "failure" and suffering; it follows the twistings and turnings of human will entangled in the double threads of selfishness and the call to serve God; it records the wrestlings of a mind awake to evidence that God's love for us and the prayers sincerely offered to Him seem sometimes to have little connection with what transpires in the world around us. So the book is the journal of a pilgrimage, a struggle of the mind in its need to make sense of the frustrations and disappointments that dog the lives of Christians and non-Christians alike. It was written at speed, because its substance had been long pondered in advance — and pondered in the face of living experience which, by its very gravity, seemed to make the writing of a book for sale in bookshops an unworthily artificial, perhaps even evasive, business. Thus the writer more than once reminds himself that, though he is tussling on paper with the problem of pain and the problem of failure, he is sitting comfortably, is relishing the interplay of argument, and has good reason to question his own right to pontificate on the spiritual demands that life's trials make on others.

Of course I had my own personal disappointments at the time, as everyone always has. For one thing, I had been writing for several years without making the impact I wished to make. I remember that C. S. Lewis wrote to me at this time commiserating with me because my trilogy of theological novels, published between June 1954 and November 1955, had been so coolly received. He spoke of his own early experience as a neglected writer and the distress it had caused him; then, fearful perhaps that his sympathy might be misinterpreted, warned me against indulging optimistic daydreams that the tide might turn. "Hope is the fawning traitor of the heart," he added. But the kind of personal disappointment thus reckoned with was not, I believe, as crucial to my state of mind as were less private concerns.

For instance, the most teasing initial disappointment to me as a theological writer was, not that I failed to produce bestsellers, but that, though there were enthusiastic readers here and there, nowhere did there seem to be a group of people who wanted to *change* the living situation in the way Christian conviction logically required. A polemical writer more easily reconciles himself to hostile disapproval than to the wrong kind of approval. There is praise which hits the ear like the kiss of the plague. And if a man begins his literary career, as I did, with an urgent call to bring Christianity and education into meaningful relationship, and then finds himself applauded for giving everyone *something to think about* by people who plainly have no conception that *something ought to be done,* then his disillusionment is something more than a matter of mere personal disappointment. The realisation that people wanted ideas as fodder for discussions and conferences, and not as impulses to action, sank deeply into me in my early days as a writer, and *A God Who Acts* no doubt bears the marks of this realisation. Indeed I think it is true to say that only when my theological books began to make a fresh impact in the U.S.A. a quarter of a century later did I become first aware of a body of readers who actually wanted to treat those books as a call to action and not merely an invitation to colloquy.

But naturally the questions probed in *A God Who Acts* took their strongest impetus from matters quite outside the sphere of writing. In my professional life I had my fair share of encounters with Christians who seemed to be doing well out of not taking their religion too seriously. The disillusionment this caused was given a bitterer flavour by ironic coincidence. For at the same time it was my lot to encounter certain tragic or near-tragic cases of men who seemed to be going through hell in consequence of taking their Christian faith very seriously indeed. There is reference to one such case in the dedicatory note prefixed to this book. Leonard Challis was a man of good social and cultural background whose vocation to the priest-hood, in which he served with great devotion, had taken him

eventually to a rather seedy, downtown parish where ultimately his mind gave way and he took his own life. He
bombarded me with massive letters during his last year, sometimes, in his disturbed condition, sitting up all night to trans-
cribe chapters of books. His case was complicated by the fact
that he had been wounded in the head during the First World
War. But it took its place among a few close objective encounters with self-sacrificial Christian suffering and "failure," to
stand in sharp contrast to what I saw in others and in myself. If
there is the authentic flavour of confrontation with suffering in
A God Who Acts, it is from these encounters that it derives.

There is no need to cite sensational calamities or to point to
particular cases of private distress in order to justify the argument tussled with in this book, for it revolves around the
Christian's most heartfelt questions of all. You cannot observe
unmerited human suffering without asking, Whatever is God
doing? You cannot pray hard for things which seem unlikely
to come to pass without wondering whether you are wasting
your time. You cannot try to do anything in the name of God
without encountering obstacles and enmities which throw
you into the kind of mental tangle which *A God Who Acts*
attempts to sort out. For the book follows with tenacity a train
of thought about God's way of dealing with His children
which is basic and elemental to the business of forcing experience and faith into some sort of logical relationship. The word
"forcing" is used because there are many souls for whom it can
be an agonising struggle to secure this relationship. There was
a point at which our Lord himself cried, "My God, my God,
why hast Thou forsaken Me?" And every Christian has to
bring his faith and his experience into coherent relationship or
he will lapse into despair, madness, or infidelity. So, following
the course of argument it does, this book is a commentary on
everyman's pilgrimage. It is a single-track book. It doesn't
turn aside from its course for knockabout fisticuffs with sec-

ularists and humanists. It continually tries to check up on its own honesty. It does not have recourse to second-hand thinking. Looking through it now, I am astonished to see how few are the proper nouns it contains; how few scholars, writers, books, or indeed technicalities of any kind are mentioned. That is because the mind is intent on following the logic of Christian understanding with a directness that leaves no room for inessentials.

H.B.
1981

PREFACE

THIS book has its origin in a series of questions. Can we define the ways in which God acts to-day upon the human scene? What is the nature of God's interference in our daily lives? These general questions are asked because (among other reasons) they relate to more personal, practical, and seemingly more pressing questions. What have we the right to expect when we invoke God's blessing upon our schemes and ventures, when we pray for his help and guidance in our personal affairs? Is the hand of God to be discerned in our failures as well as in our successes—in failure, that is, not only to fulfil private ambition or to satisfy personal desire, but to carry through worth-while schemes entered upon for the good of others, and even entered upon in the name of God himself?

In the present intellectual climate, the attitude to questions like these is peculiar. The modern mind regards such questions as starting-points for discussion, as fuel to set in motion the free-play of intellectual interchange: it looks upon them as mental cocktails, to loosen our tongues, stimulate our brains, and warm us up to a pleasant, companionable party-game in which ideas blossom and breed to the general enrichment of our mental life. The modern mind, in short, sees such questions as the fodder for discussion in conference, study-group, or private gathering; but it does not in the least anticipate that the questions will be actually answered. Indeed, in the minds of some of our contemporaries, we detect a positive apprehension lest such questions *should* be answered; lest the human brain should be robbed of the delights of exploration by being bereft of problems and equipped with conclusions.

Now a truly disquieting fact about the Christian Faith—a literally disquieting fact—is this: that if you press your questions within the framework of revealed truth, proven experience, and the canons of reason, you will inevitably arrive at clear answers. And the nature of these answers is noteworthy. For, not infrequently, having arrived at them, you realize that they have taken you further than you wanted to go. You almost, perhaps actually, regret that you ever raised or grappled with them. This is not an uncommon experience for the reader (or the writer) of religious books. Having ventured, in a truly modern spirit, to ask and press certain questions about God and his ways, eventually, in the course of reading (or writing), he discovers to his dismay that God has answered them. It is not quite what he wanted. He looked, perhaps, for the delightful intellectual stimulus of playing off notion against notion, experience against experience, in a pattern of dancing ideas. He looked for all the pleasures of discussion and argument, the balancing of thesis and counter-thesis, and the peculiar delight of demolishing the errors of others. But, as he proceeds with his work—writer or reader—he finds that God has entered into the matter in his effective and unmistakable way. His entry provides the answer—nay, his entry is itself the answer. There is no more to be said: but a great deal to be done.

This pattern of experience is, of course, a familiar one in the Christian life. If we seek God earnestly, we shall find him—or rather, he will find us. If we ask God humbly to come into our lives, he will indeed come. And he will not do with us what we had expected—still less what we had "hoped". We shall find, to our dismay as natural men, that the God whose assistance we remotely invoked is already here, within us, speaking, even commanding; his presence manifested in an immediate and imperative revealing of duty and obligation. We asked him to advise, to help, to strengthen, from afar. He comes to in-dwell, command, and direct, within.

That this rhythm of experience applies to our intellectual inquiries as well as to our strivings to live the Christian life is one more proof that God's truth is active and dynamic—a personal, living thing, and not a set of static, impersonal propositions. It lends to all our intellectual researches in the theological field a faint air—not perhaps of triviality—but of failing to get to grips. It pushes us back from study to prayer, from our chair at the desk onto our knees before the altar. Above all, I think, it adds to the deep gravity of our theological argument, to our vehement denunciations of heresy and error, a faint echo of divine laughter—laughter neither derisive nor ironic, but tranquil, rich, well-pleased. That we should have followed such a long, such an arduous course, in order to arrive at this simple living contact with him who gives himself to the wise and simple, the learned and the unlettered, in like fullness and abundance!

Nevertheless we must make the long journey, because we cannot deny the nature he has given us as rational men; because the ending of the journey is different from the setting-out by virtue of every toil and hindrance encountered and overcome on the way; because our journey's end is always, by definition, the end of a journey, though better a thousand times than the zest of travelling hopefully is the settled joy of arrival.

1

GOD'S PLACE AMONG US

ARE CHRISTIAN teachers and apologists too ready with their answers? Do we make crucial statements of Christian truth too glibly, too eagerly? Do we sufficiently take into account that a statement or an exhortation will persuade or compel only if the receiver is in a frame of mind appropriately adjusted to reception? These questions occurred to at least one listener when he heard on the radio a few passages from a recent Quiz programme, in which, amid discussion of this and that, eternal truths of Divine Revelation were pithily—even chattily—summed up by an eminent ecclesiast. For we must admit that this readiness with answers has never been the way of the world's great teachers. Consider Socrates, for instance. How long and laboriously he worked upon his audience before he brought out a compelling proposition directly expressing his own conviction! What patience and perseverance there was in questioning and counter-questioning before the moment arrived for uttering the conclusive truth! And how these truths gained—in persuasiveness, force, and authority—through being dug laboriously out of the soil of error and half-truth! How memorable and compelling it made them, this process of discovering them like hidden remains, and not distributing them at random like advertising leaflets.

This proves how deeply Socrates was aware of that difficulty in communication which some of our contemporaries seem to treat as a newly-discovered problem in the world of thought.

And a very little analysis of Socrates' technique of persuasion in the Platonic dialogues will show how his elaborate manipulation of his auditors served to put them into the frame of mind in which truths—perhaps unpalatable truths—could be accepted wholeheartedly, their compulsiveness depending upon their sheer relevance to the questions at issue. This criterion of relevance is crucial. R. G. Collingwood has argued that a statement can be fully understood and judged only if one is aware of the question which it answers. True answers are not enough. They must be matched with appropriate questions. In these days when, in the realm of Christian apologetic, we hear so much about the "Christian answer" to this and that, it behoves us to ensure, not only that the answers are true, but also that they are correct; not only that they are consonant with the Christian Faith, but also that they are strictly in accord with the questions asked.

It is possible that a great deal of Christian apologetic misses fire through carelessness in this matter. If we are going to give our contemporaries the right answers, we must first ensure that they ask the right questions. In an age marked by apathy, rather than by hostility, to the religious issue, it is perhaps more immediately important to put questions into the minds of our contemporaries than to try to put answers there. Indeed it is useless to distribute answers to people who are not asking questions. We who try, in the pulpit or on the printed page, to bring the Christian challenge before our countrymen, must be wary lest we fail, not through lack of zeal or fervour, but through sheer inadvertence. If it is morally grievous to fail through lack of zeal or fervour, it is faintly absurd to fail through inadvertence.

Perhaps it is unnecessarily far-fetched to drag in Socrates for our pattern in this matter. A little acquaintance with the gospels will suffice to prove that our Lord himself was economical in direct public persuasion. It might be a valuable piece of work

to examine the circumstances which our Lord chose for uttering direct dogmatic propositions. There were occasions when
a compelling public utterance came as the climax to an act
which had already shaken his hearers out of complacency and
self-trust into a state of dependence and acceptance. Thus our
Lord taught directly in public after the raising of Lazarus and
after the cleansing of the temple. Consider what must have
been the state of mind of those villagers who had seen the
stinking, buried corpse of Lazarus walk shrouded from its
sepulchre: and compare it with the state of mind of the modern
audience which now, in hall or home, receives the truths of
God from the lips of a clergyman sitting cheek by jowl with
the rationalist and the atheist on the Quiz platform. Again, we
may be sure that those citizens of Jerusalem who had seen the
Carpenter from Nazareth hound out the money-changers from
the national temple in a whirlwind of righteous anger—we
may be sure that they had more amazement in their hearts and
more questions on their lips than the quiet congregation last
Sunday at Evensong.

Of course our Lord did not teach only in the atmosphere of
the miraculous and the sensational. He taught under the sun
on quiet hill-sides. But then he dealt in parables, preparing his
hearers' hearts and minds, not like Socrates by ruthless probing
and merciless exposure, but by giving them stories illustrative
of the human situation for which his teaching catered. Before
forgiveness and reconciliation, all the waywardness, ingrati-
tude, and selfishness of the prodigal's career through vice and
dissipation. Thus have great teachers prepared the hearts and
minds of their hearers before uttering direct truths and exhortations. We have reason to suspect that our Lord would not have
consented to sit on the Brains Trust; that Socrates would have
been an unruly member of the Quiz team.

Are our contemporaries generally in the appropriate frame
of mind to receive direct religious teaching? Are they asking

the questions which Christian preachers and apologists are answering? Let us follow our own advice and put this issue in the form of a concrete illustration before we resort to direct utterance.

John Smith is 26. He has been married two years. If all goes well, he hopes that in a year or two his wife will be able to leave her job so that they can start a family—but not a big one, for economic reasons. Not that they are in any financial difficulty. On the contrary, the double income is giving them a very promising start in married life. John is a clerk in the local authority's offices. By working conscientiously and being pleasant to everyone, he hopes to be able to rise a few grades during the next thirty-five years. There is reasonable hope of promotion, and consequent increase in salary, twice or three times in his future working life. This is very pleasant to contemplate. On the employment front, the picture of life is secure and reasonably hopeful. A lucky fluke might even at some date push him right to the top in the office; but, even without that, prospects are fair enough. A thirty-five-year span of earning his living in tolerable comfort lies before him. On the home front things are equally comfortable. John and his wife live in a new council house, equipped with all modern conveniences. They have recently acquired a television set. In a few more years they should be able to afford a car. Meantime Mrs Smith is a good housewife who knows that a man likes tasty meals, warm rooms, and comfortable chairs. John follows the local soccer team at the week-end. He fills in his Pools coupons regularly, but with the sensible restraint characteristic of him. He and his wife like the cinema. They have one or two good friends of their own age. Life is not busy, but pleasantly full. From Christmas one looks forward to the annual summer holiday. After that one looks forward to Christmas again.

What must be stressed is that John's picture of life is a comfortable one, a secure one, and—even so far as the conscience is concerned—an untroubled one. Old age is a long way off, and anyway John's superannuation scheme ensures that, with luck, his latest days will but extend the easy tenor of his way. His own parents are very contented in the little bungalow supplied by the council. John will admit that his own post enabled him to fix this up neatly; but then any man of sense seizes whatever opportunities his particular job provides for easing the lot of his own family. On those rare occasions when John's wife drags him to Evensong, he hears nothing which disturbs his complacency. On the contrary, he takes solace from the fact that numbers of sensible, educated men are apparently quite convinced that a happy home hereafter awaits us when we die. For this is the kind of thing he most readily takes in from the pulpit or the hymn-book. There is a great deal else which passes him by. Either he fails to understand it, or he thinks it is irrelevant to his case—which amounts to the same thing.

For instance, suppose the parish priest talks about sin. John listens, but the personal application eludes him. He assumes that "sin" means the kind of thing for which people are put in gaol and, like the priest, he is all against it. Perhaps he reflects wistfully on the story of some acquaintance who lost his job in a bank through a little adventure in embezzlement; and he pats himself on the back for his own prudence and honesty. Or suppose the priest talks about suffering. Again the personal application eludes John. He thinks his sympathy is being sought for a few rare and remote individuals who have had exceptionally bad luck, thus missing that equable tenor of life which he unquestioningly regards as the norm. The very word *suffering* strikes him as something alien and other. He confidently assumes that it will never belong to himself personally. As for phrases about the "godless rush and distraction of modern life", he takes them for indirect lamentations on the press of traffic in our roads and the danger it occasions to life and limb. Again, he assumes that sermons which dwell on the wickedness and selfishness of twentieth-century men are veiled attacks on communist Russia; while general references to life's pains and horrors are received as allusions to a possible third world war.

It is by no means entirely John's fault, this personal blindness and insensitiveness. He has been conditioned to a picture of life which excludes the spiritual, ignores God, and cushions the soul against challenge and self-scrutiny. He has been conditioned by modern education, modern journalism, the radio, and television. Strife, pain, death, disease, privation, and even evil itself, he regards as abnormalities—things which, if they strike you, get you into the news, because they offend against the prevailing pattern of comfort and well-being. They are one and all outside John's personal picture of his own life, framed as it is by State-subsidized security and the insurance of general welfare. Hence, when John sits before the pulpit, there is an unbridgeable gap between speaker and listener. For the priest who addresses John on those rare Sunday evenings, suffering, disease, death, sin, and privation are all firmly within his picture of life. They are a part of the lot which he recognizes as inevitably his own by virtue of his very humanity. Not only are they daily within his knowledge of what other men endure; they are daily within his vision of his own personal course through life. He knows that he has sinned, that he will suffer, that he will die; knows it as something felt and realized. These burdens are actualities, not hypothetical possibilities remote from the immediate prospect. In short, the priest's picture of life is utterly different from that of his auditor, John Smith. In so far as the priest preaches a faith which caters for men who suffer, sin, and die, he preaches a faith which John Smith, in his present frame of mind, will never begin to understand, let alone receive. He has not been prepared for such a faith. Many devices of modern education, entertainment, and propaganda have been exploited to ensure that he should not be prepared for such a faith, He is therefore a long, long way from asking the questions which the priest is patiently answering.

We have heard a great deal since the war about the obstacle to Christian evangelism represented by the hostile *climate of opinion*, which generally rejects the idea of the supernatural. *Climate of opinion* is indeed a useful phrase to describe the popular notions current in our society. By this phrase we denote the vast number of vague presuppositions about the nature and meaning of human life and the ends which individuals and societies ought to pursue, which seem to underlie popular thinking in moral, social, and political affairs. We detect among these presuppositions—the superstitions of our age—notions which are quite clearly watered-down versions of propositions which belong to the great intellectual heresies of our age—psychological determinism, naturalism, and materialism. We observe that the great heresies have spread from the intellectuals to the masses, seeping down through the mental life of our society by means of organized education, journalism, and mass-entertainment. Having observed, we put our finger on these crucial heresies, noting how they have spread so as to infect the prevailing consciousness of our age with *a priori* prejudices against the spiritual and the religious.

There is no doubt that the diagnosis of popular thinking which I have just described is a sound and useful one. Certainly the masses are infected with notions that have their roots in the intellectual infidelities of the scholars. But growing experience leads one to doubt whether this much-vaunted anti-religious climate of opinion is as potent or profound an obstacle to Christian evangelism as many apologists would have us believe. The claim made here is that something which we have called the *picture of life* is a graver enemy to Christianity than the popular climate of opinion.

At first sight it will appear that to substitute the phrase *picture of life* for the phrase *climate of opinion* is merely to

7

play with words, but the distinction has been made thoughtfully, and our intention is to press it home. For the phrase *climate of opinion* suggests, in however diluted or distorted a form, a body of rational propositions in the background. It suggests a hostility to Christianity with a rational content which, at least when expressed by the learned, is intellectually respectable. The phrase *picture of life*, on the other hand, is meant to suggest a state of mind and a set of attitudes which have no rational basis of any kind, a state of mind and a set of attitudes which, if he were challenged, the intelligent rationalist would deplore as readily as the Christian.

The question before us, therefore, is this: When we come face to face with the apathy of our contemporaries to the religious issue, are we up against diluted materialism and diluted naturalism, or are we up against something which is wholly irrational at its very centre? The question is an important one. It may be that we spend far too much time in attacking heresies which, precisely because they are dimly understood, are correspondingly weak in their influence. If popular apathy is fundamentally irrational, we do wrong to dignify it by according it an intellectual status to which it has no claim. May it not be that we do too much honour to the materialistic and naturalistic philosophers by assuming that their utterances sway the minds of the millions? It is not for us to exaggerate the influence of anti-Christian thinkers, and to accord them an authority over the contemporary mind which in fact they do not possess.

What is meant by the phrase *picture of life* has already been roughly sketched out in our illustrative account of John Smith's mentality. John Smith is more or less indifferent to religion; but it would be absurd to accord his indifference the status of a rational objection. He is too concerned about his personal comfort and physical well-being to recognize the challenge of the Gospel; but it would be wrong to confer the exalted title of "materialist" upon him. Far from being a materialist, he cannot be said to have any philosophy at all. For to have a philosophy—even a naturalistic pagan philosophy—is to accept a rational basis for action which takes all possible contingencies into account. But John Smith takes nothing unpleasant into account at all. For one thing, he has too little imagination. He cannot therefore be said to be, in any serious sense, infected by the philosophy of materialism. John Smith's central concern with his own comfort and well-being is not philosophical at all: on the contrary, it is plain selfishness. And the difficulty in approaching him with the Christian message resides, not in the fact that our age is infected with erroneous philosophies, but in the fact that human beings, now as always, are too much at the mercy of their selfish appetites and passions.

Have we, then, overestimated our enemy? I think not. We have done him too much honour; we have accorded him too much respect as being of an intellectual nature; but we have not overestimated him. On the contrary, we have probably underestimated him, for there are no foes to truth so powerful as the selfish passions. Beside them the force of intellectual error is weak indeed. John Smith's picture of life takes no account of sin, suffering, and death. That is a central deficiency. No doubt intellectual heresies—the popular climate of opinion —have helped to produce the situation in which such a picture of life can mature, unchallenged and unscrutinized. But the crucial obstacle to faith which this picture of life presents is a moral rather than an intellectual one, a matter of sin rather than a matter of error.

This does not mean that we have to deal merely with a disposition of the will and not with a state of mind. We most certainly have to deal with a state of mind. But this state of mind—this picture of life—is fed and sustained chiefly by moral weakness (by selfishness); it has no deep roots in the intellectual heresies of the learned. In short, if we wish to investigate the mental, as well as the moral, aspects of modern man's religious apathy, we shall have to introduce categories with no truly reputable philosophical ancestry.

The picture of life which takes no account of sin, suffering, and death: that is what faces us. What is its basis, and how is it sustained? If it has no respectable philosophical basis, what are the modes of thinking which enable it to "satisfy" the mind? We can see why and how it satisfies the appetites and passions, by the total exclusion of the unpleasant from the sphere of familiar reference. To construct one's total and operative vision of personal life around the artificial securities of a welfare economy and the prospect of acquiring more and more of the distracting devices fabricated for our comfort and amusement by modern technology—this is to while away the span of morality in a continuous day-dream. That so many forces, even forces supposedly cultural and educational, operate towards the sustaining of such a day-dream, is a grave matter: but our concern at present is not so much with the external as with the internal problem. And the internal problem—the problem of what takes place inside modern man's heart and head—has both its moral and its mental aspects. The difference between the two must be clearly noted. The moral condition is an old one. The state of mind is perhaps a new one.

First for the moral condition. Men have always coveted and lusted, sought for themselves the comforts of security, self-indulgence, and sloth. Men have always desired to possess the novel and superficially attractive article. There is no moral difference between wanting for yourself, above all other things, a spear like your neighbour's and a television set like your neighbour's, between coveting an ornamental suit of armour and coveting a glossy Ford Zephyr. There is no moral difference between neglecting your duties through a passion for jousting and neglecting them through a passion for dog-racing.

Thus if modern life has given us new opportunities for self-indulgence and forgetfulness of duty, it has also taken others away. True, I can choose between three or four neighbouring cinemas for my entertainment this evening: but I cannot go out to watch cock-fighting, bear-baiting, or gladiatorial bloodshed.

Thus, in so far as modern man's attitude to life is morally deficient, it merely subscribes to those selfish appetites and passions which men in all ages have found no difficulty in serving. We cannot believe that any particular generation is handicapped in the moral contest through being presented with an excess of temptations over opportunities for good. We know that every good thing contrived by hand or brain offers corresponding opportunities for use and abuse. The car can be an instrument of service or of selfishness. So could the horse and the chariot. The opportunities for unchastity provided by the West End in the 1950s certainly do not exceed those provided by the South Bank in the 1600s. A car may enable you to chase a girl more remorselessly: it may also enable her to get away from you more expeditiously.

Let us then turn from the question of modern man's moral condition to that of his state of mind, studying it the more carefully, not because it is cogent or rational, but because it is perhaps new. We have said that the increasing security of contemporary urban life does not bring increasing moral temptations—or, if it does, it compensates for them by bringing increasing opportunities for service. It has, however, bred a state of mind insusceptible to the religious appeal in a quite distinct and very disturbing way. And here one gropes fumblingly for terms adequate to express a feature of the twentieth-century popular mentality which has never received the attention it deserves.

Perhaps we can best define this feature by saying that modern man's picture of life has a *quantitative* rather than a *qualitative* basis. Now Christianity insists upon a qualitative estimate of experience. It is axiomatic that sincere Christians, however halting their progress in the spiritual life, are deeply and daily conscious of good and evil. They are continually engaged in making value-judgements—not necessarily, of course, acting wisely and virtuously after making them, that is a different matter. But we may agree that the professing Christian, conscious of his Christian allegiance, is quite unable to refrain from making judgements of value upon the systems, schemes, projects, personal and impersonal, individual and social, which he encounters in his daily life. Good and evil are his prevailing standards of reference. The fact that his awareness is acute, even among stumbling Christians, is borne out by the accusation that Church people are prone to faction and gossip—a charge which, even if true, is not without its "hopeful" side. For there is no doubt that keen awareness of good and evil may stimulate faction and uncharity where spiritual discipline is weak or fitful.

The point to be stressed here, however, is that growth in the Christian Faith inevitably sharpens ever more keenly man's sensitiveness to the conflict between the powers of light and the powers of darkness, pervading every human endeavour, private and public, manifesting itself wherever men gather together, whether to work or to play, whether to construct or destroy. Thus the Christian, according to the degree of light that is within him, categorizes every act and event that he encounters, perhaps every turning of a head or lifting of an eyebrow, under the one heading or the other. His developing Christian conscience—which is not the same thing, of course, as his personal taste or inclination—approves or disapproves. The Christian is trained in value-judgements. As for variations in degrees of charity, that is a different matter with which we are not immediately concerned: but the Christian looks out upon his world with an essentially *qualitative* mode of vision.

What, then, do we mean by saying that modern man's picture of life—the popular, post-Christian picture of life—has a *quantitative basis?* Simply this: that modern man thinks, not in terms of good and evil, but in terms of the normal and the abnormal. On the mental—as opposed to the moral—plane, this is the very heart and core of that contemporary apathy which is wedded to urban security. We call judgement in terms of the normal and the abnormal *quantitative* because it is rooted in the majority-minority dichotomy, and indeed we must perforce recognize it as one of the less desirable products of the "democratic" mentality. Of course it must be understood that we are here investigating something which is never explicit, a mode of thought which is neither conscious nor coherent, and not susceptible to precise definition. Nevertheless, if we investigate, for instance, the widespread use of the barbarous word "normalcy" in the materialistic press during the years immediately following the war, we shall find our case both corroborated and clarified. And the characteristics which apparently constitute the norm turn out to be the following: peace, health, employment, a sufficiency of money, well-insured security, the possession of a convenient modern home, the gradual acquisition of more and more worldly possessions, especially gadgets for the house, a plentiful supply of free and cheap entertainment, and so on. In making this list, we are not of course making any comment upon the value of the things listed as proper aids to a full life. That many of them are in themselves good things goes without saying. And for the mentality that we are investigating the norm is automatically the criterion of desirability. Thus the corresponding list of characteristics which constitute the abnormal (or the exceptional) would be: war, disease, unemployment, poverty, homelessness, deprivation, suffering, and of course death.

If we wish truly to see from the inside the popular picture of life held by our contemporaries, I do not think we can over-estimate the potency of this categorization into the normal and the abnormal. And two effects produced by this way of think-ing concern us here. One is the fact that it precludes value-judgements over a very wide area of experience. Thus, in the popular mind, the man who questions the true value of any of the products of modern technology is assumed to be unbalanced.

But, quite apart from this question of evaluation, there is another great difference between surveying the human scene in terms of good and evil, and surveying it in terms of the normal and the abnormal. Let us take war as our example. By seeing war as primarily an evil thing, we inevitably put it in the same category as evils closer and more personal to ourselves —perhaps our besetting sin of irritation and bad temper. This brings a true quality of war home to us. We *realize* it. We even, to some extent, assume a responsibility in relation to it. But by seeing war as primarily an abnormality, we set it at a distance. We discount it in drawing our picture of life. We put it outside the frame of things in which we are involved, and for which we are in a measure responsible. In the same way, by regarding poverty as an evil thing, we relate it, as no doubt it should be related, to evils more personal to us—our own sins of wasteful-ness, extravagance, and self-indulgence. By being "placed" in our evaluative scheme, it shows itself to be linked to our own hearts and wills by a thousand threads of momentary self-interest and fitful charity. But to regard poverty as an abnor-mality is to put it outside the pattern of experiences which touch us. We discount it. Thus there are only two alternatives. Either we shall realize the evils of life, or we shall forget them. Either we shall learn to see ourselves tied to each one of them in a tangled net of guilt and responsibility, or we shall, per-haps gradually, lose any effective awareness of their existence.

Nothing is easier—we dare scarcely ask how perilous it is spiritually—than to sit in an armchair and to accuse our contemporaries of being forgetful of suffering, evil, and death. We have only to tour the local council estate, and we shall no doubt come across a hundred instances of homes heroically held together in the face of some crushing blight like blindness, paralysis, cancer, or bereavement. But it is rarely in homes like these that one finds characteristic twentieth-century apathy. And any honest attempt to diagnose the spiritual and intellectual temper of our age will inevitably have to reckon with apathy and unthinkingly selfish contentment on an enormous scale. We have only to look into our own hearts to realize that. And indeed every sincere attack on human weakness reflects a self-castigation: that goes without saying. The evidence of our own spiritual poverty and moral weakness is enough to prove how readily, under the pressure of organized and advertised security, we push suffering and evil outside the frame of our picture of life.

We must not yet take leave of the distinction between the normal and the abnormal. We are going to need it badly later on. The claim made here is that this distinction sums up a mode of thinking now generally current, which is an inflexible obstacle to Christian evangelism. John Smith, in the secrecy of his own soul, has calculated arithmetically that the chances of his being knocked down by a bus are slight, that the chances of his dying at the age of 35 from tuberculosis are slight—so slight as to be negligible. Indeed the average man's mortal prospects have been officially supplied—almost guaranteed—to him by an expertly calculated table which gives him his "Expectation of Life". And here indeed we touch grave matters. For it is not possible to dwell for long on this quantitative picture of life without realizing the damage done to the twentieth-century popular mentality by the spread of so-called statistical information in the spheres covered by sociological, psychological, and educational research. Here is "knowledge" whose acquisition and surveyal never call a single value-judgement into play. Here is fact-gathering totally divorced from the exercise of wisdom or judgement. Here is an allegedly "scientific" system of surveying experience arithmetically which grants to the average and to the norm the honours and dignities of democratic predominance.

In an age in which even the human intelligence is measured arithmetically, it is surely not far-fetched to claim that quantitative judgement has run riot—especially since this system of measurement itself depends unashamedly, not on some ideal standard of "the intelligent", but simply on the drab dominion of the statistically average. Our argument here suggests that the popular picture of life "democratically" rules out of count the statistically negligible, under which heading it categorizes disease, suffering, disaster, and all the accidents of mortality. That is to say, our popular mentality rules it out as a likely personal prospect. At moments when complacency is temporarily disturbed by some comparatively close acquaintance with an instance of the "abnormal", then we restore our confidence by taking out a modest insurance policy in self-protection. The very lavishness of the Insurance Company's provisions against a possible personal encounter with tragedy guarantees the extreme unlikelihood of our realizing it.

Communication of the Christian challenge is possible only against a mental background which takes suffering, sin, and death into account, which *realizes* them. As long as we hold them centrally within our sphere of familiar mental reference, we cannot turn a deaf ear to the deepest intrusions of the living Word. But as long as these tragic realities of human experience exist nebulously and remotely on the shadowy fringes of our sphere of familiar reference, we can fob off the spiritual challenge. Taking refuge in the heavily-insured security of the glorified statistical norm, we set ourselves at a distance from tragedy. When a blow falls in our immediate neighbourhood, we tremble for a moment, touch wood, and return hurriedly to the routines of our familiar security.

"Security is mortal's chiefest enemy." Certainly the false security of feeling ourselves thoroughly and for all practical purposes, as we say, at home in this middle earth, is the great impediment to faith. For it is the thing which most impedes the growth of any human sense of dependence: and the sense of dependence is the ground of faith. Has the Welfare State aggravated our insensitivity to the true insecurity of mortal life? Perhaps so. But there is no good thing which cannot be abused as well as used. No Christian who knew our mining areas in 1938 and saw them again in 1948 will rashly cast a stone at the Welfare State. Neither reason nor honesty will allow us to forget that there is now greater justice and equity in this country than there ever was before. It is the best things that can be most vilely corrupted. It takes a beautiful woman to make a really successful prostitute.

Christian evangelism is now called to break into minds whose scheme of things has no place for it. God—and this is the crux of our argument—God is not denied, but, as an active Person, he is relegated to the sphere of the abnormal, the exceptional. Religious experience is not denied; that prayers are occasionally answered is willingly believed; but the religious phenomenon, whatever its nature, belongs to the sphere of the *exceptional*. That is the prevailing assumption; and many of our contemporaries are willing to take out a modest insurance policy against the practically negligible likelihood of an encounter with God in the foreseeable future. Hence the occasional attention to a broadcast service, and those few personal returns to the fold for baptism, marriage, and so on. But, viewed as an expression of the popular state of mind, these little safeguards are almost on a par with other more commercial safeguards against possible personal disaster.

Now if this theory of quantitative estimate represents a true diagnosis of our popular state of mind, it explains much that is otherwise inexplicable. For instance, we are bewildered, not by hostility, but by the odd combination of friendliness and apathy towards the Church. The friendliness is due to the fact that God's existence and activity are reckoned with. The apathy is due to the fact that God's activity is regarded as an altogether exceptional matter. It happens, but only very rarely. That is the response to the priest's patient instruction in fact and doctrine. It is true, but of course it hardly ever applies. That God answers the prayer of some rare, unfortunate individual at the very extremity of his sufferings and the utmost crisis of his endurance—that is firmly and generally believed, and we must thank God that it is so. But that God acts frequently, daily, hourly, within the sphere of human life—that idea is not entertained for a moment.

Indeed, if this is so, we can see why there is no hostility to the claims made for God. There is no hostility for the simple reason that, when these claims are made, they are believed. But they are believed in a very peculiar and limited way. They are taken within the framework of a state of mind which immediately and automatically categorizes them as belonging to the sphere of the abnormal, the rare, the exceptional. They are true, even in a sense important, but fortunately for the most part they just don't apply. Not to me, because I am a normal sort of man living a normal sort of life. Good? Evil? Well, not really either; just normal, not doing much in the way of positively charitable acts, but certainly not getting on badly with people. Even (alas) "good" and "evil" are terms largely irrelevant to my daily activities. For most of the time (fallacy of fallacies!) I am not being either—just being normal. You say Christ died for sinners, and I take your word for it. It was a fine and noble thing to do. And indeed it will be a comforting safeguard for me to remember that, if ever I cease to be normal and become that exceptional thing, a sinner. You say we are all sinners, and of course that, in a sense, is true: for I remember stealing a shilling from my mother's purse when I was 9, and I went too far with that girl after the dance on my twenty-first; but fortunately these are exceptional instances: my normal level of behaviour has been—well, normal.

How, in Heaven's name—literally in the name of Heaven—can one break into this state of mind with the Christian truth? For every truth that is uttered is received, but received after a fashion of receiving that nullifies its potency. Every proclamation of the Gospel message is believed, but believed in a mode of believing that emasculates and kills. God incarnate walked the earth—but that was during a most exceptional period twenty centuries ago. Martyrs have given their lives for the Faith—but in what remote and exceptional circumstances! Even now God may speak, act, give a sign, in answer to pressing human need at some moment of tragic crisis or disaster—but how peculiarly unfortunate are those rare men and women whose odd taste or destiny brings them to such an exceptional pass! How desperate, how tragic, is a man's situation when, all other resources exhausted, he is thrown back upon eternal God! That is the attitude that confronts us to-day. The acts of God are known—but on the very fringe of things knowable. The knowledge of God's power is stored in the memory along with other data accumulated against a possible rainy day—the location of the nearest police-box, the vital phone number, 999. But immediately applicable? Relevant to me, here, now, alive, healthy, free, untroubled? Thank God (yes, even thank God!), no.

What, then, must be said? Anything, anything that imposes the utmost pressure of moral quality and spiritual reality upon the slightest acts of daily life. You cannot lift a hand or raise your eyes to another without doing a good act or an evil act. You cannot spend sixpence in a shop without doing a good act or an evil act. You cannot pass the salt across the table without fulfilling God's will or opposing God's will. You cannot wilfully eat a mouthful of porridge but in virtue or sinfulness. In every act, every movement of your daily life, you are God's child, obedient or disobedient. In your every thought, every plan, every uttered word, God is active or God is resisted.

Perhaps we have moved too quickly to the direct statement of a Christian truth which belongs more properly to a later chapter. If so, our motive was the justifiable one of trying to give a cutting edge to truths much blunted by our own ingrained unresponsiveness. God is not on the fringe of life: he is in the dead centre, at every moment resisted or obeyed. Under his eye there is neither neutrality nor normality: there is only good and evil, obedience and disobedience, surrender and rejection.

Progress through life—if it is progress in wisdom—is marked by a strange opening of the eyes, a progressive adjustment of our focus upon the field of human experience. For every grave event that touches us personally seems to remove one more feature of human experience from the fringe of our vision of life to its centre—from the sphere of the exceptional, if you like, to the sphere of the normal. (If we are logical, we gradually realize that a category which is progressively being whittled away will eventually cease to be a category at all.) We will not take physical pain as our example, because many of us escape the experience of acute physical pain until late in our lives. We will take failure, for if we strive after anything at all, considerable or inconsiderable, we eventually come to know the taste of failure. Disappointment over the outcome of some earnest and sincere endeavour is surely familiar to most of us, and its lessons can be readily appreciated.

In the experience of failure, the hard discipline of events gradually teaches us that the thing we put on the very fringes of our field of personal awareness—the possibility of failing in what we most ardently wished to achieve—has got to be moved into the very centre of our field of reference. That is a crucial and necessary development. If we do not make this adjustment at the proper time, "facing the facts" it is called, we give ourselves up to day-dreaming of an escapist kind. If we do, then that realization of disappointment which, when we began to strive, we consigned to the remote outskirts of our calculations, is shifted to the very heart and core of our own personal vision. There it has to be—not just savoured—but consumed and digested.

The first effect of the experience of disappointment is to teach us to put failure into the very centre of our personal realizations. At that stage only half the lesson is learned. We have brought failure from the outskirts of our personal encounter with life to the centre of that encounter. But still we may regard ourselves —we probably shall at first—as exceptions, illogically proving the golden rule. At that stage failure makes us feel to be chosen victims, the objects of ill fortune which is exceptional, abnormal. It may be that we never pass beyond this stage. Some people never do. They develop a persecution mania, a peculiar form of inverted vanity. But men of sound judgement gradually learn from their own failure that others fail too; that all who strive earnestly are conscious of failure to some extent, even those whose external achievements strike the world as impressive monuments to success. In short, one thing that the life of continued effort and reflection teaches us is that the failure we thought exceptional and abnormal is in fact normal and general. We learn that life is just like that: not my life only, but life in general. Wherever we turn in serious reading or conversation, we find confessions, admissions, and lamentations which echo the sense of failure which we had thought to be peculiarly and exceptionally our own.

The rhythm of this experience illustrates a general law of life, which might have been equally well illustrated by the experience of pain, or by some notable joy or profound illumination. Note that two corresponding developments have been described together. For progress in life—if we are earnest and reflective—is marked by the shifting of sorrows and joys from the outer fringes of our experience and our calculations to the centre of our realization of life (a personal encounter) and to the centre of our picture of life (an intellectual construction). Now the Christian believes that the discipline of this development is God-given. He recognizes, as the experience proceeds, that God is using it in order to change both his realization of life and his picture of life. He is also uncomfortably aware in the back of his mind that, if he does not learn the required lesson from this particular discipline, God, of his unquenchable love, will provide another and yet another discipline until the lesson is truly learned. That, however, is a different issue, and belongs to developments of the argument to be found later in this book. Meantime we must concentrate upon the apparent law of life by which we are compelled gradually to embrace in proximity what we first regarded as alien and remote, to examine under a microscope what we first chose to survey through a telescope.

What lessons, then, are we learning? This: that we had no right to put disappointment on the fringe of our realizations. It belongs in the centre, firmly grasped in our embrace. And— a far more frightening question— what lessons *shall* we learn? In God's good time (may it be a long way off!) this: that we had no right to put pain on the fringe of our realizations. It belongs in the centre, here, locked in the grip of fingers which only God can keep clenched and firm. And—it is terrifying even to write it—this lesson too we shall one day learn: that we had no right to put death on the fringe of our realizations. It belongs in the centre, here, grasped, scrutinized, stared in the face—this thing which God has not yet given us strength to contemplate even from a distance.

Now this law of life applies especially and supremely to our awareness of God. We have consigned God to the fringes of our field of awareness, actual and intellectual, and he demands to be in the centre. Thus, when we spoke of modern man's habit of relegating God to the sphere of the exceptional, we were describing a state of mind which, in greater or lesser degree, belongs to all of us. And the whole process of conversion and progress in the Christian life consists in allowing God to move from the outskirts of our daily calculations and encounters to the centre where knowing and greeting meet.

It is one thing to say that, another thing to do it. It is easy to speak of allowing God to walk into the centre of our lives, but hard and bitter indeed to remove a single barrier that stands in his way. It is so much harder to do than to say that saying itself seems a kind of blasphemy. Only the saint can speak or write of the Christian way, allowing the argument to run its logical course, without reaching the point at which he wonders whether it is to his soul's peril to add the next word. Only the doctrine of inspiration can save most of us from the silence of shame. This we dare not say. This we are not fit to say. But this God says himself through us.

God must be in the centre, where knowing and greeting meet. And is not this, after all, exactly what the Incarnation itself involves? God walked into history. History had put him on the outskirts of its busy life, and God walked into the centre. History—human history—had to embrace him: he was there within its arms. History did embrace him, with the murderous embrace of the bear at bay. The bear knows his human enemy and crushes the life out of him. History knew its divine enemy —the foe of all its meaningless cycles of grasping and losing, vanquishing and succumbing, constructing and destroying; the foe of every assertive impulse to possess and dominate by which the wheels of history turn and grind.

Yet, you will say, that is only part of the story. God, by his very presence and pleasure among us, enriched and transfigured that sphere of the natural which was itself outraged at his coming. Of course. Every utterable truth about God is only part of the story. But what an important part this is, that tells us the way of God with men, that tells us how he will walk into the very centre of our personal lives, there to be grappled with as the foe of our self-centredness, to be embraced within the pressures of a self-protective grasp that squeezes from his broken body the drops of his redeeming blood.

The pattern of God's ways with men: that is the whole theme of this present book. Yet no progress can be made in exploration of this theme until this first point is fixed in the heart and mind: that the pattern is not something which he works out from a distance: that his way is not the way of the overseer, the fabricator, the back-room administrator. God does not sit at the nerve-centre of operations with a dozen telephones on his desk. God walks into the centre—the centre of human history in his Divine Incarnation, the centre of human worship and endeavour in his Church and her sacraments, the centre of the individual's heart and soul through the grace which he bestows. God is unfailingly relevant—the eternal, inescapable point of reference at every movement of hand or brain.

The centrality of God. How easily the phrase slips from tongue or pen. And what a fine, fetching title for a book, a sermon, or a week-end conference in a comfortable seaside guest-house! Now that it has indeed become—through no direct intention of the writer's—the subject of a book, how tempting to keep it as that, just that. An idea to be developed, embroidered, illuminated by analogy and illustration. A theme to make the reviewers say, "A book that will make you think." But God forbid that Christian truth, however it reaches us, should merely make us think! The centrality of God is the end of thinking and the beginning of action—of prayer, surrender, self-committal. The centrality of God will bring the unexpected, perhaps the cataclysmic. It will mean, perhaps, for the reader the end of reading, for the writer the end of writing. We do not know. Perhaps that is another costly thing to be learned—something just around the corner when the last sentence of this book is written or read. Perhaps the entry of God into the very centre of our lives will mean for us the end of reading or writing religious books which enable us to play with the Divine Truth in words, balancing, measuring, shaping the unfathomable Revelation at the same intellectual level at which we discuss the latest play or the latest novel. We do not know. But we must be prepared. For God will not come to terms with our unregenerate assertiveness, however loudly it asserts his Name.

2

THE PATTERN OF GOD'S WAY

IN THE earthly events of God's incarnate life we have the
pattern of God's activity at the human level. That fact has
always been recognized in Christendom, though frequently
it has been misunderstood and false deductions have been
drawn from it. For instance, to say that our Lord's earthly
career presents us with the pattern of God's activity is not the
same thing as to say that it presents us with the pattern for
man's activity. No doubt there is a sense in which the latter
assertion is true as the former; but it is true only in a subordi-
nate and derivative sense. To regard our Lord's earthly career
as though it were primarily and supremely significant as a
model which we ourselves ought to imitate is certainly to put
the cart before the horse, and perhaps to be guilty of a blasphemous presumption. Exemplarism, the heresy which over-
looks or understresses our Lord's redemptive work, making of
him essentially and primarily a model for us to imitate, has
always had a wide vogue on the fringes of Christian com-
munions, and even more so among those who claim to be
Christians without involving themselves in the life of the
Church. Nevertheless this heresy has been condemned by orthodoxy in all ages.

We see this heresy at work when our Lord's passion and self-
sacrifice are recommended as simply the perfect pattern for
human behaviour—an inspiring lesson in the virtues of patience,
humility, fortitude, and self-giving. Now of course our Lord's

earthly career is a pattern for us in the sense that man has seen nothing better done by man, and never will. But we grossly misread God's way with men if we regard the earthly career that culminated in the great redemptive act as simply a proto-type, set before us so that we should, of our own wills, construct careers corresponding with it, having no community of sub-stance with it, yet perfectly matching it in detail.

The heresy of Exemplarism is easily recognizable in its ex-treme form; but, like all heresies, it can infect individual faith in small doses, obscurely and covertly; and indeed it does so in our own day on a very considerable scale. Only the grace of a healthy faith can defeat it in practice. Only cool logic can refute it in theory. It is therefore necessary to stress, at the beginning of an investigation into some of the "meanings" of the Incarnation, that it is primarily and essentially a pattern of God's activity, not of our own. Here, once more, we see how necessary it is to ask the right questions. We shall miss the essential meaning of the Incarnation if we approach it by ask-ing, "What does it teach me about my duty as a Christian?" instead of ,"How does it express God's way with man?"

The Incarnation, then, is the pattern of God's activity, and the word *God's* is crucial. But so is the word *activity*: for the incarnate life of our Lord is more than a revelation of God's *nature*; it is a revelation of his *behaviour*. We learn from it, not primarily what God is, but what God does. In making this point we are once more, of course, correcting a half-truth, not combating a falsehood. For, as Aristotle tells us in the *Poetics*, character is expressed in action. Nevertheless it is important to get the emphasis right from the start, for a false emphasis here can lead us gradually into another grave heresy. It is a very respectable heresy in England. On the whole it is rather more respectable than mere Christianity: and for a weighty reason. It is the heresy which men educated in the classical tradition most readily incline to, the heresy of those who, in their school-days, have been fed on Plato and the Gospels side by side.

A very modest familiarity with the Platonic philosophy develops in the young a deeply poetic sense of the way in which the temporal order manifests the qualities of an eternal order beyond the reach of change and decay. Alert to the opening wonder of life, the young readily respond to the good and the beautiful in nature and art and human beings, as expressive of an infinite reality which will never fade. By an easy and logical transference of thought, the person of our Lord is seen as the expression within time of the divine and eternal Personality. All this is sound so far as it goes. It is right and proper that the wisdom of Plato should be put at the service of the Christian Faith, for indeed it provides us with concepts and categories that enrich our interpretation of the incarnation. But we must not turn the relationship between Plato and the Faith topsy-turvy. We must not put the Christian Revelation at the service of Platonic philosophy, to crown its illuminations with the supreme instance of Absoluteness embodied in finite form. The danger of a faith dominated by Platonism, rather than served by Platonism, is that the dynamic character of God's activity is overlooked. The earthly career of our Lord becomes a mere static symbol of a particular kind of perfection—something to be contemplated, rather than something to be shared in. More-over the Platonic emphasis confines the Gospel revelation in its historical context. This revelation was given to us as the symbol of the most perfect and personal God. We hold it before our eyes like a work of art, a spectacle which can inspire us and from which we can learn. This, of course, is not enough; and it is not surprising that the practical effects of Platonized "Christianity" are on a par with those of pure Exemplarism. Our Lord is praised, imitated, even worshipped: but the call to share in the living activity of God is not heard.

Our Lord's earthly career, then, is the pattern of God's

activity. Indeed we may say that in itself it proves that God is an *active* God—that he is that kind of person and not another kind; that he is the kind of God who acts. Have we even now felt the full force of that? That the God whom we worship in church on Sundays, whom we call upon in our daily prayers, is known for a certainty (in the only sequence of events in which he is properly known at all) to be the kind of God who *acts*? The weight of meaning within this truth is enormous, almost unbearable. Suppose we introduced an intelligent Buddhist, who had never heard of Christianity, to the Gospel revelation. What would be the first thing to strike him about the nature of this Christian God? What sudden realization would constitute the first overwhelming impact with reality, the first astonishing collision with novelty? Not, I think, that this is a God of love: not that this is a God of self-sacrifice: but that this is a God who does things.

When we say our prayers before getting into bed, are we deeply conscious of calling upon a God who acts? Not a God who can be occasionally and reluctantly stirred to action by the pressure of some distant yet persistent human appeal, but a God whose nature and whose joy it is to be ceaselessly, tirelessly active? For it is the first thing we are told of him, that he made the world and enjoyed making it. And the first announcement of the Gospel narrative is not a proclamation about his nature or even his demands. The Angel Gabriel comes to tell our Lady what God is going to do. It is not recorded that he made any introductory remarks about God's nature. That was not necessary. God was to be revealed in action. It was only needful to say that with him nothing is impossible. That is the first "Christian" description of God—one whose powers of action are illimitable. As a first axiom it would not have satisfied Plato. As the primary premiss of faith we too readily forget it. But we can learn from our Lady's response. Not—Behold God's creature, willing to worship him: not—Behold God's daughter,

29

full of respect for him. No, that is too static: God is already busy. Behold God's handmaid, ready to be used by him in his active work.

The work is already afoot. God initiates: man fits in with his plan—or he does not fit in. We speak of God's answer to prayer, and what an unfortunate phrase it is. How much damage it can do, used so frequently and so glibly. As though the rhythm of divine activity on earth usually started with man. As though man were the initiator, conceiving a desirable course of action, bringing it to God's notice as one might send a letter to an M.P., and then waiting for a favourable response— hoping, as we say, that the idea will be adopted. God is always active. If we have a good idea—a really good, unselfish idea— then indeed he gave it to us. It was his before it was ours. We cannot give him anything he has not given us. The perfect prayer is always our Lady's prayer. Be it unto me according to thy word.

Man fits in with God's plan—or he does not fit in. Our Lady was obedient. But—it must be said with reverence—Mary, wife of Joseph, was not indispensable. If she had not obeyed, God could have found another. And, whatever views we hold about the degree of devotion due to the Virgin Mary, her status as the object of veneration must always and inevitably be qualified by this fact, that, as a human creature like you and me, she was not indispensable to God.

We have now learned our first lesson from the Incarnation as the pattern of God's activity among men. He is not the kind of God who is laboriously pressed into action by human prayer, stirred from passivity by ideas submitted from below. If we pray to him as that kind of God, then we pray to him as something which he is not. He is an initiating God. His incarnate encounter with humanity is a dramatic action whose plot was conceived in heaven, not a piece of cosmic legislation pushed through the high courts in response to human petition. Is that the kind of God we prayed to this morning? Or did we, perhaps, pray to another God, one whose angelic herald would speak differently: "At long last God has decided to answer the earnest appeals of his people for salvation from sin and death. Touched by the prayers of his faithful children through many centuries, he has now decided to make clearly known to men that he is a God of love and forgiveness"? It could so easily, we feel, have been that. A comforting proclamation wrung at last from the eternal throne. An official message of assurance, meriting three cheers and a vote of thanks from long-suffering humanity. But it was something far different. God will do this and this and this. It is your human duty to fit in.

It would seem to follow logically from all this that the Church, if she is truly God's incarnate Body upon earth, will not be primarily a teaching institution whose main duty is to distribute descriptions of God for the enlightenment of men. She will be primarily an active body. Her most fundamental call will not be: "Come here, that you may learn what is the true nature of God", but rather: "Here, among us, God is at work, using his children. Come and be used as he intends you to be used." This fact carries inescapable inferences which will disturb our complacency. If the Church is first and foremost God in action rather than a world-wide university faculty in theology and morality, then the primary call to the outsider does not invite him to learn about God, but to play the part assigned to him by God. The distinction is important for this reason especially. The call to learn implies that the outsider is at a disadvantage through his ignorance. The call to play a part assigned is more provocative. It implies that the outsider is disobedient.

Are we, for the most part, up against ignorance? Or are we up against disobedience? I mean in ourselves as well as in others. It is tempting to believe that ignorance is God's main enemy on earth. Tempting, because it enables us to satisfy our consciences by reading books like this: worse still, perhaps, because it enables us to satisfy our consciences by writing books like this. With every new chapter there is the temptation to write some such heading as *The meaning of the Incarnation*. With every fresh paragraph there is the temptation to begin— *What we learn from the Incarnation is this or that*. All very right and proper, of course, provided that the sphere of knowledge is clearly defined and distinguished from the sphere of obedience: but so very dangerous and potentially misleading too. For the first thing we "learn" is that God acts and we are involved: not that God teaches and we are his pupils.

We must not regard the Divine Incarnation and the Redemption as essentially a *mode of teaching*—a universal morality play setting forth the abstract quality of virtue and godliness through the media of allegory, symbolism, and personification. The startling events of our Lord's incarnate life do not constitute, in their primary essence, an aptly illustrated lesson in divinity. There is something quite blasphemous about exhortations which treat the solemn events of Bethlehem and Calvary as though they were a teaching device divinely chosen for its capacity to impress the senses and brains of finite creatures. There is also something faintly, almost comically, absurd about this attitude. For—if it may be said without irreverence—a divine birth in a cheerless stable and a crucifixion at the side of criminals represent a cumbersome, even clumsy, mode of instruction. No, the unparalleled sweep and stir of the Gospel narrative do not represent God the teacher. They manifest God in action. Everything in contemporary preaching and teaching which confers an essentially illustrative, anecdotal status upon the incarnate life of our Lord is gnostic rather than truly Christian.

The second crucial point about the Divine Incarnation is that it *is* an incarnation. God acts on earth; but he acts in man. And here a double significance must be emphasized. Firstly, God operates within human society, not remotely from above. He is among men. Secondly, God operates as a man among men; not simply as a God among men. The mode of God's operation is within the human sphere. The mode of God's operation is within the human being.

Is that the kind of God we said our prayers to this morning? Not a God who will intervene from afar, but a God who will act at our side and act within our heart? Is this the God to whom we forwarded that petition that we should be preserved from a pressing danger or delivered from the sin of uncharity? Not an eternal Sovereign, presiding at a supernatural privy council, who will lay a decisive finger on the human programme mapped out for to-day or to-morrow; but a God who will enter into this situation at my side, in my heart; perhaps even at my enemy's side, or in his heart. And even that does not go far enough: for God is already in the situation, reckoned with or ignored, already in my heart, obeyed or rejected.

Here again our notion of God suffers from one of the false modes of thinking referred to in the previous chapter. Whilst admitting and marvelling at the manifestation of God in Christ, we yet tend to think of this manifestation as *exceptional*. As though God acted, for once, rather out of character. By emphasizing—as we rightly must—the uniqueness of the Incarnation, by pressing home the paradox of Divine Self-emptying, by stressing the sheer pathos of Omnipotence humbled in the manger and humiliated on the cross, we encourage in our minds a half-conscious attitude which it is difficult to clinch in words, but it amounts to this. The Incarnation is seen as an almost reluctant concession on the part of a God driven to extremity by the growth of human sin, a desperate recourse to a means which only desperation could bring into play. Now of course the Incarnation is exceptional in the sense that it is unique: but it is not exceptional in the sense that it shows God acting out of character. We miss a central significance of the Incarnation unless it provokes from us the response, "So that is the kind of God he is!"

Not, therefore, "He is the kind of God who loves humanity so much that *he lays aside his true nature* in order to come to earth and bring salvation to men." No; rather, "He is the kind of God whose nature is best expressed in his coming to earth and bringing salvation to men." He acted in character. That was his way, his chosen way; not the regretted, uncharacteristic expedient of one trapped in a narrow strait; not even the wild, impulsive throw of the dice when all, and more than all, seems lost already; but his chosen, wished-for way. It is unthinkable that God, in revealing himself, should reveal himself out of character. It is inconceivable that in Jesus Christ we catch a glimpse of God on one of his off-days, as we say. There is self-emptying. Omnipotence confines itself within human flesh and blood. But that does not mean that God is temporarily behaving in a ungodly manner. It means that true godliness is other than we should otherwise have thought it. We too readily think of our Lord's incarnate life as God's self-imposed sentence of exclusion from Godhead. It is not easy to think of the just illustrative analogy: but suppose we picture Bach, say, abandoning his organ for some charitable and self-sacrificial purpose, and wheeling a hurdy-gurdy round the streets, turning the handle to the rhythm of vulgar rag-time. In no sense is the Incarnation like that: for the essential feature of Bach's hypothetical humiliation is that it is out of keeping with his character, wishes, and capacities. But God's Incarnation is the accurate expression of his character, wishes, and—if the incongruous word may be excused—his capacities.

He is a God who operates among men and within man. Moving among men, to what extent does he perform actions which are openly and indisputably beyond the range of any merely human capacities? We think of the miracles, of course.

THE PATTERN OF GOD'S WAY

In any consideration of God's mode of acting upon earth, the miracles must be taken into account. It is probably true to say that there is something paradoxical about the different ways in which the miracles strike believers and unbelievers. To the unbeliever the miracles are a stumbling-block. What astonishes him about them is precisely their miraculousness. But the believer takes a different view. He is astonished that God in Man so consistently avoids the overt sensational miracle. There are exceptions, of course; notably the raising of Lazarus, which was witnessed by a considerable number of people. But, generally speaking, there is a remarkable lack of fuss. There is no summoning of legions of angels: lightning is not called down from Heaven: crowds are not entertained by supernatural phenomena. On the contrary, our Lord seems to be determined, without resorting to concealment or subterfuge, to make his miraculous acts, as nearly as can be, consonant with the natural processes of human life. It must seem to many that one of the most authentically divine notes struck by our Lord during his earthly career is that double restraint evidenced in his miracles. For it is a double restraint. On the one hand, our Lord eschews the paraphernalia of the sensational supernatural sign. Even when feeding the five thousand, he does not call for manna from Heaven, but carefully gathers in the available resources of bread and fish. On the other hand, our Lord restrains himself from the conscious concealment: he does not resort to any pretence that what he does is a purely natural and human achievement. The Man does not play the God. The God does not play the Man. The God-Man acts.

There is a corollary to all this in the life of the Church. God's incarnate life continues among us in the Church which is his Body. He will act in and through the Church: he will act in and through its individual members. There will be no sequence of sensational miracles in the life of the Church: neither need we assume that the miraculous will be excluded from its manifestations. We have every reason to expect the quiet miracle, neither elaborately staged, nor masquerading as the purely natural. In the life of the Church God will not pretend not to be God. Neither will man, if he is wise and humble, pretend not to be man. And here we touch the very heart and core of much inter-denominational controversy; for if it is treachery for the Divine Body to play at being merely human, it is blasphemous for the human institution to play at being God.

We have earlier explained that behind everything said in this book stands a group of questions. They are the questions which this book sets out to answer. Some of them we have already grappled with—What kind of a god is our God? In what way has he shown his hand in human history? Others will emerge as the argument proceeds. But one which is peculiarly relevant to this stage of the argument may be framed thus—What kind of thing have we the right to expect when we ask for God's blessing upon our friends, or upon our own schemes and ventures; when we pray for God's guidance and help upon others or in our personal affairs? We must expect that God will act in accordance with his revealed character, and this we have begun to study through thinking about his earthly Incarnation.

God being the God we know him by revelation to be, we recognize that a petitionary prayer is not a request for intervention from afar, but a request for activity within man and through men. We shall not expect the miraculous sign: neither shall we expect God to pretend not to be God. We are dealing with a God who acts; but it would be foolish to say that we shall expect that God will act; for we know that he is acting already, even acting in our act of prayer. When we pray, even in petition, we do not initiate. God is always the initiator. If we are praying for something which is in accordance with God's will, then we can be sure that he is already operating towards the end we pray for. Does this make nonsense of petitionary prayer? I think not. Even on the level of ordinary human relationships it would not be so. It is not nonsensical for me to say to my friend, "I hope you are feeling better", even though he knows already that I wish him well in all things. It is not nonsensical for the child to ask his mother for the piece of bread which he knows she would not deny him.

We have said that petitionary prayer is inevitably prayer for God's activity within men. Since we can pray for nothing better than that men should be obedient to God, it follows that we can pray no better prayer than that God's will shall be done. Does this severely limit the prayers we can with propriety utter? At first sight it might appear that it does; but on further reflection it will be proved not to do so.

In the first place, there is much that we can pray for which we know for a certainty to be in keeping with God's will: the conversion of sinners generally and of certain sinners in particular; the spread of the Gospel; the faithfulness of God's ministers; his blessing upon those who preach, teach, heal, and so on. But quite apart from prayers which clearly and directly accord with the will of God, the matter is simpler than it might appear. Unless one is consciously perverse, it is not at all easy to pray against God's will. I am not sure that it is even possible.

Let us take the kind of example that frequently disquiets religious people. Suppose X is grievously ill. I love X. I decide to pray for his recovery. Is it possible that I may be praying against God's will? (We will assume that X is a young man. We are surely sensible enough not to pray automatically for the "recovery" of the old.) Now we know that God uses sickness as an instrument, a means by which souls may be disciplined and saved. We know that sickness has brought repentance and faith to many a man who in health neglected God. Suppose X's case is an instance of disciplinary sickness. God has given him this illness that he may be drawn nearer to himself. Is my prayer for X's recovery prayed against God's will?

There are two replies to this question. In the first place, if God has made X sick with the intention of disciplining him, it may well be that God intends to restore him to health if and when the discipline has been effective. In that case my prayer for X's recovery (though I presumably do not know it) is a prayer that the discipline may be effective. I am praying for what God himself desires—X disciplined and restored to health. For, in a case of this kind, we may assume that God deplores the sickness *qua* sickness, however much he desires the possible fruits of sickness. We must not pretend that this explanation covers all cases. We can be sure that it does not. There are cases in which men are called to share in the physical suffering endured by our Lord himself in the crucifixion. This is a positive vocation. And therefore it is necessary to give a further explanation, showing another sense in which my prayer for X's recovery is in accordance with God's will.

There is nothing obscure or complicated about this second explanation. Indeed it is simple, yet irresistible. We are all God's children. God wills that I should love X. He wills that I should desire X's well-being with all my heart. He knows what that means in human terms. It means that I must pray for X's recovery. Indeed, paradoxical as it may sound on the surface, this conclusion is the only one that logic will allow. If we are dealing with a loving God, as most certainly we are, then he wills that *I* should pray for X's recovery, even if he does not himself will X's recovery.

We have not yet answered the question posed above: What have we the right to expect when we ask God's blessing upon our friends? In the strictest sense, of course, we have no *right* to *expect* anything. That is to say, we must not look for some external sign. To do so, perhaps, betokens a lack of faith. But, as Christians, we assume that our prayer for our friend's good is taken up and involved in God's own purposes for the good of our friend. In so far as our prayer is truly for the good of our friend, it is *wholly* in accord with God's will, no matter with what degree of misinterpretation we cloud the issue for ourselves, by assuming that we know exactly what is best for our friend. Thus prayer for a friend's well-being inevitably has the character of an act of obedience to the divine will, even though ignorance may frame the request in a form which God rejects. In short, as long as we are praying for others, we are praying for others, and thus, in some measure, endeavouring to put our wills into accord with the divine will. The fruits of our prayers will be produced, in some form or other, *within* the lives of those we pray for. Frequently there are surprises, so that we say God moves in a mysterious way. Thus prayer for X's recovery is perhaps followed, not by an improvement in X's health, but by a new reconcilement to sickness in X's heart, or by a new access of penitence and faith.

We are in a better position to measure the results of prayer when we have prayed for guidance and help in our own personal affairs. Here we find indeed, as experience generally testifies, that God acts through men in response. How often, after praying sincerely for help on the brink of some deep despair or infidelity, we receive the answer unexpectedly from another—staring at us from the middle of a page in that book which,. on the strength of an apparently meaningless impulse, we happened to select from the shelves of the public library; or thrown at us from the pulpit at that service which only at the last moment we had decided to attend. That is typical of the Christian's experience: and in our more careless moments we are tempted to dismiss it as fortuitous coincidence.

Let it be said firmly that, applied to significant events, the whole notion of fortuitous coincidence is diabolical. By describing an event as a coincidence, we declare that event an extreme instance of chance. But from the very core of the

Christian message we learn that we are not in a world dominated by chance. We are in a world operating under God's own
purposes. A chance event is an unpurposed event: that, and
nothing more. To assume that our lives on this earth are,
generally and in detail, under no purposeful divine governance,
is to believe that God has abdicated, withdrawn, or fallen
asleep. There is no place within the Christian Faith for an
absent God in whose created universe events happen hap-
hazardly and meaninglessly. For—there can be no mistake
about it—a universe governed by chance is a meaningless universe: and perhaps the first axiom of Christianity in its judgement upon the human situation is that life is not meaningless.
The suddenly encountered sentence, read or heard, which unexpectedly illuminates our way, which dispels a cloud of despair
or dismay, which gives meaning to what before seemed meaningless—that is never coincidence. It is Divine Providence.
Wherever and whenever we find our experience suddenly rendered meaningful, by whatever human agency, there and then
we encounter the will of God.

Is this superstition? On the contrary, it is the only logical
deduction from these rational premises: that God acts; that he
is purposeful; and that he loves us.

The word *chance*, when it is used of grave or momentous
events in our lives, is a dangerous word both spiritually and
intellectually. It saves us the trouble of thinking. It enables us
to shirk our duty to see life as meaningful and to make it
meaningful. By using it, we rob potentially fruitful occurrences
of their true significance, and reduce them to the level of the
trivial. We have no right to put sudden blows or sudden delights, sudden insights and illuminations, on the same level as
throws of the dice in Ludo or Snakes and Ladders. To do so is,
for all practical purposes, to leave our world bereft of its
Creator and Director. The instinct which leads man to posit
a tyrannous Fate, dominating his days through a fixed pattern

of pre-ordained weal and woe, is healthier and humbler than the irreverent pretence that life is chaotically meaningless at its very centre. And, once we reckon with an operative force behind human history and human aspiration, we have to deal with the supernatural in one form or another. Destiny, God, or Devil: between these three we must make our choice in assigning an extra-temporal source to events which have the superficial character of unmotivated blessings or banes. And since the concept of Destiny, being a symbol of irrational will, is merely what we call *chance* personified and divinized, then if we believe our world to be meaningful, we shall have to interpret in terms of God and the Devil.

What, then, are we to make of a great natural disaster? Suppose an avalanche buries a village, killing hundreds of people. How far can we go in asserting that a disaster of this kind is an expression of God's will? In the first place, the avalanche itself is an expression of God's will in the sense that he gave the natural order its laws of operation. In the second place, the consequent destruction of human life is in accordance with God's will in the sense that he has willed men to live within the scope and reach of natural accident in exactly this way. It is certainly part of his divine provision for men that they should always live in possible risk of sudden death. This is one of the "natural" disciplines which he has imposed upon all humanity. He has imposed it out of his love for us, in that he wills us to be deeply aware of our dependent finite status. He gives us these incentives to wilful dependence upon him, these encouragements to set our hearts surely on what is reliable through change, accident, and death. Thus every natural disaster is both meaningful and generally expressive of God's concern for men and his purpose for men. That, as Christians, we perhaps believe the death of each separate person in a case like this to be individually and particularly an expression of

God's purpose is an additional thesis superfluous to our argument.

It would perhaps be a pity to press this additional thesis. The doctrine of Providence does not require us to do so. It does not claim that every misfortune (even every natural disaster) is divinely purposed; only that it is divinely purposeful. There is a great difference here. We have no right to claim of any given misfortune (especially another's misfortune) that it is directly expressive of God's will: only that it can be made an instrument for the expression of God's will. There is something impious (not to say unhelpful) in assuming that the crippling of your neighbour's child by poliomyelitis specifically shows God's hand at work.

The distinction between that which is divinely purposed (directly so) and that which is divinely purposeful, is difficult only because our point of view is that of finite creatures subject to time. We can readily imagine—though we cannot exactly define—how this difficulty falls away for those who truly achieve the eternal point of view. But, keeping within the idiom of the temporal, we may say that meaning is retrospective. We accept this principle in considering our Lord's incarnate career. We read the cross into the Christmas story, and the Resurrection into the events of Good Friday. Meaning is always supra-temporal in that it grows in that continuity of consciousness which we call memory, and reflects back upon past experience. Spiritual meaning, of the kind that concerns us here, is the backward reflection of obedience. Thus it was our Lord's obedience unto death which gave the true meaning to his incarnate birth. In this sense—though on a totally different level of achievement—our own obedience will give spiritual meaning to those things which touch us most momentously, however tragic their nature. And what exactly do we mean by *spiritual meaning*? Simply this: that by our obedience we shall learn to see even our misfortunes subsumed into the pattern of God's good purposes for ourselves and for all men. And once we have found God's Providence thus operative, and even our misfortunes rendered meaningful, shall we any longer trouble to ask whether the particular misfortune in which (temporally speaking) the pattern of obedience began, was itself directly expressive of God's will? The question has itself become meaningless as the experience has become meaningful.

The overall purposefulness which faith gradually discerns at the heart of things leaves no room for chance as a potent factor in human affairs. And while chance, as an operative force, is gradually obliterated in our survey of the human situation, the dominion of Providence, in general and in detail, assumes ever greater power and significance. Perhaps no idea is so desperately in need of rehabilitation within Christendom as the idea of Divine Providence. Through the weakness of our faith, the idea of Providence has suffered a vulgarization which has all but robbed it of meaning. "The hand of Providence!" we say, when some remarkable event gives a new turn to circumstances after the eleventh hour has struck and some overwhelming tragedy seems imminent. Is not this the very error already attacked in this book; the error of assuming that only on rare occasions of extremest urgency does God interfere in human affairs? "Providence has intervened", we say with a sigh, as a life is saved by inches in a road accident. No doubt Providence *did* act. But must we say *intervene* of a God whose hand is daily and hourly upon the affairs of men? Must we speak as though God only occasionally wakened up to the cries of human distress, to make a quick saving sally into the world of men—like a guerilla warrior operating in enemy territory— thence to retire immediately to his long sleep of neglect?

In our use of the word *Providence* we sum up the fact that God is ceaselessly active among men and within man. And the measure of his activity (or at least of our responsiveness to his activity) is seen in the fact that experience is rendered meaningful. God being both active and purposeful, it follows that his touch in human affairs always operates towards the fulfilment of his general design. What his general design is has been made known to us in our Lord's Incarnation and in the teaching of the Church. His design is that men should love and glorify him in freedom and in truth, learning to live, even while upon this earth, within the kingdom of love over which he rules through all eternity. In prayer, unless we pray in utter selfishness (and that is not true prayer at all) we express, in one way or another, our fundamental dependence upon God, and to that extent bring ourselves consciously and wilfully within the operative pattern which he has designed for human beings in general and for each one of us in particular. God wills precisely this: that we should fit into his design consciously and freely. It follows that he wishes us to experience, in full awareness, the joy of his service. And to rejoice consciously in the service of God is, since we are rational human beings, to *realize*, in some measure at least, the part we are playing in his great design.

Having said that, perhaps we are in a position to answer quite clearly the question posed a few pages back—What have we the right to expect when we pray for God's help and guidance in our personal affairs? We have the right (the logical, not the moral, right) to expect that our experience will be rendered meaningful (though not necessarily meaningful according to earthly standards of judgement). This is surely the most constant and telling fruit of petitionary prayer on behalf of ourselves. We pray sincerely for God's blessing upon some personal scheme or venture. By earthly standards it fails completely. But, provided that we continue to pray, in submission to God's will, that our efforts may be blessed, the fruits of this creaturely dependence will undoubtedly emerge. And they will emerge in the form of a new realization of the meaningfulness of the part we are playing. It may be that the whole of our striving, which we perhaps undertook for the benefit of others, has been used by God primarily as a spiritual discipline for ourselves, in which failure plays a crucial part. We thank God for his love for us which has effected this development. We find ourselves rejoicing over the failure of that scheme on which we had set our heart. It may be that God has used the experience to teach us that we are not indispensable, or that he has used it to show us that, when we thought we were acting altruistically, we were really serving our own wills in consciously "virtuous" self-assertion. Or it may be that the failure of some plan is quite simply and directly a corrective. Although we undertook it from the first conscientiously believing it to be the right course, it is now revealed to have been the wrong course. Our ideas of what we ought to do, or how we ought to do it, have been quite plainly corrected. In so far as we set out anxious to do God's will, we acted to God's satisfaction. But man is free—other men as well as ourselves—and it may be that the circumstances of our upbringing and education have together given us the wrong picture of the way to act in God's service. When our scheme fails, if we pray sincerely and submissively, we shall understand what was erroneous in our conception and method of service. Corrected, we try another, better way of service. What then? Why, our ideas may still be twisted, perhaps through no fault of our own; for education sees to it that the sins and errors of the fathers shall be visited upon the children unto the third and fourth generation. In that case, the pattern of failure and correction will be repeated until we learn the true way of service.

The consideration of personal petitionary prayer inevitably involves this close analysis of failure and disappointment. For if prayer is "successful", there is no problem. If I pray sincerely, and in submission to God's will, for his blessing upon some particular act or scheme, and that venture is richly blessed in its outcome, I have every reason to believe that God's purposes have been served. It is easy to rejoice then in God's service. So easy that God will fulfil this pattern with very few of us, and that only rarely perhaps. Few of us have achieved that high degree of self-surrender which can "stand" continual success in the ventures we undertake, even those undertaken consciously in God's service. God loves us too much to shower upon us, as a result of our prayers, the very circumstances that will most readily feed our pride, vanity, and self-dependence. Do we not, if we pray at all, pray daily to be delivered from temptation? This prayer God answers in abundance when he denies continued successes to those who are only beginning to learn to serve him. This, your daily prayer, God answered for you only last week, when you failed to get that promotion you sought, when you failed to sway that meeting in favour of your plan—so right and godly a plan it was!—when (if the layman may fitly say it) you preached your best, most pondered sermon of the last twelve months to an almost empty church. He delivered you from evil. He led you not into temptation.

Once more, however, this does not mean that every failure you experience is itself a direct expression of God's will. If you set out, in good faith, to convert a sinner, and you fail completely, that failure obviously cannot be accounted an expression of God's will. Yet this does not mean either that God has been defeated—nor that you, as God's instrument, have been defeated: for there are aspects of your failure which can be spiritually fruitful, for yourself, and perhaps for others later on. In other words, the Christian doctrine of Divine Providence is not fatalistic. On the contrary, it introduces into every situation, joyous or tragic, an element of purposefulness. It does not teach you to say of every disappointment, "This had to be: it is God's will"; but rather, "Even in this God's will can be done and his good purposes manifested."

That was God's way during his incarnate life. The defection

46

and treachery of Judas did not defeat him: nor did the judgement of Pilate and the hatred of the Jews. If there is an obedient human instrument to hand, there is no situation in which God's will cannot be in some way manifested. Given a single obedient human will, God's good purposes can be shown forth amid the extremest assaults of blasphemy and rebellion. Fortunately for most of us, we are not likely to encounter anything physically dangerous in the way of assaults upon our faith. Our society does not go in for bloody martyrdoms. But the numberless minor trials which beset the believer in post-Christian England can together constitute quite a searching test of obedience. And sometimes even the intelligence is sorely strained in the effort to define how our grotesque difficulties can be made to bear any fruit at all. That is our peculiar burden as twentieth-century Christians. In a civilization so lopsidedly and perversely cerebral, we must expect the obedient brain to be teased.

God acts on earth: he acts among men and within man: and he acts in self-sacrifice. That is our third deduction from the facts of our Lord's incarnate life: God does not, in the worldly sense, act successfully. He does not advertise his omnipotence by using his power to justify his claim: he does not work towards the open proclamation of indisputable sovereignty: he works towards the self-sacrifice of the Cross. Again it is logical to believe that, in acting self-sacrificially, God acts *in character*. Also, of course, we believe that, in acting self-sacrificially, God acts *freely*. Both these points—aspects of the same truth—are important, for they can correct misreadings of the Incarnation and the Redemption.

What we said about the divine self-emptying which is effected in the Incarnation, applies equally to the divine self-sacrifice represented by the Redemption. These acts of God are in character. They are not excursions into eccentricity which belie the true, established nature of godhead. They are not novel experiments in modes of behaviour alien to divinity. They are at the very heart of the Divine Identity. Thus, in meditating upon the crucifixion of our Lord, we must not exhaust our wonder by exclaiming, "That God himself should wilfully abrogate godhead to that extent!" Rather we must say, "So that is the kind of God he is. That, then, is the true nature of godhead!" The prime marvel is, not that God should stoop from godhead to self-sacrifice, but that self-sacrifice should be the characteristic activity of godhead.

It is also the *freely chosen* activity of godhead. If we picture God as one who is driven to extremities by the perils of a situation which has got completely out of hand, we are in danger of limiting God's own freedom and omnipotence. If we picture God driven to the desperate act of self-sacrifice after a wringing of the divine hands at the eleventh hour of human peril, then our Lord's redemptive work takes on the appearance of an extorted and uncharacteristic act. Observe that, in putting this notion into words, we have twice spoken of God as being "driven". As applied to God, the word is meaningless. There is no one to coerce God. Certain emphases, in speaking of our Lord's self-sacrifice, half-consciously presuppose the existence of some omnipotent Fate whose demands God himself must satisfy. Of course a satisfaction is made: and to obliterate any idea of satisfaction is to weaken the doctrine of the Atonement. Nevertheless it is a satisfaction which God *chooses* to make. He is that kind of God.

It matters. It is relevant to us every day of our lives that he is that kind of God: one who chooses to act on earth and among men in self-sacrifice. Surely there is no statement to be made about God which removes more difficulties than this one removes; real difficulties, not theoretical problems faced by the intellect, but hard actualities of practical personal experience; pain, disappointment, frustration, failure. It is in these modes that God acts among us.

THE PATTERN OF GOD'S WAY

Perhaps now a point made in Chapter I will be clearer. It is necessary for us to take pain and disappointment into the centre of our experience precisely because they are in the centre of God's experience. Suffering does not lie on the fringes of God's awareness, but at the core. We are not permitted to believe that God reached out once, and only once, from his familiar sphere of comfort and complacency to grasp the nettle, danger, on behalf of despairing man. He is not a God whose realization of suffering is occasional and fitful: for suffering is eternally a chosen mode of his love for man. He does not momentarily stretch out a divine arm from a throne of glorious reposefulness, to touch the thorn of man's disquietude or test the blade of human pain. The thorns are his familiar crown, and the sword pierces his heart. This follows, if God's incarnate course was in character. This follows; that God embraces suffering and makes it his own.

God does not temporarily *condescend*. He does not stoop, making periodic excursions from the exalted immunity of godhead. There is no exalted immunity to take a holiday from. He is not that kind of God. He has chosen not to be immune. That is the character—the prevailing, unvarying character—of his godhead. You cannot condescend, except from a position of prevailing, assured exaltation in immunity. God has forsworn immunity. What does the Incarnation mean if not that God has forsworn immunity? The king who rises from his throne to greet a poor old lady, his subject, that king condescends. But the king whose established practice it is to live and suffer among his humblest subjects, he has got beyond condescension to a new realization of sovereignty.

God chose to act within the finite framework in rejection of divine immunity. He chose to work, from the human point of view, towards unsuccess. Is that the kind of God we prayed to this morning? A God who acts at the human level towards suffering and self-sacrifice? Is that the God whose guidance we invoked upon ourselves this morning, whose spirit we prayed for that it might dwell in our hearts, whose very life we asked to share in. A God who enters into this, my present situation, and guides me out of it to the hill-top of Calvary; a God-in-man whose uttermost spiritual resources were gathered and disciplined to self-immolation, whose life was a prologue to the spending of blood?

Or did we perhaps pray to another God—a God whose prevailing character it is to pat men on the back and grant them in abundance the fulfilment of their earthly desires? Did we perhaps pray to that extraordinary God who, while he expresses his own love in agony and self-sacrifice, chooses that his children should express theirs in a continuous round of self-fulfilments? Did we pray perhaps to that truly incomprehensible God who chooses for his sinless Son the way of suffering, and grants to his sinful sons the realization of all their cherished earthly dreams?

It is important that we should pray to the Christian God, and not to a God of our own devising. It is important, but it is neither easy nor (in the earthly sense) stimulating. For the Christian God chooses the action of suffering. And when a rebellious voice within us cries out, "Ah, but he is the God of Love!", the Church, if she is faithful, has only one answer: "Are you sure that you know the nature of Love?"

A major curse of contemporary Christendom has been the replacement of traditional theology by a new system which we may call *Twentieth-century Sentimental Theology*. Sentimental theology has invented a God: it insists that he is a God of love, and implies that it is therefore his eternal concern that a thumping good time should be had by all. Are we in the dumps? Pray to this God and, at a word, he restores us to self-confident buoyancy. Are we living in a society torn by factions and dissensions over questions of practice and principle whose roots reach down to the depths where angel and demon are locked in conflict? A word with this God of infinite forbearance, and we shall be granted the dubious capacity to face all-comers, friend or foe, with the same inscrutably acquiescent grin. Are we worried about this hypocrisy or that dishonesty, about this injustice or that treachery? Five minutes of prayer to this many-sided God, and we shall be able to rejoice indiscriminately with sinner and saint; we shall be able to spread the family spirit of Christian charity like a blanket over every disloyalty and in-fidelity conceived in Hell and planted in men's hearts.

So runs the Sentimental Creed. Because this God loves all men equally, therefore we must live in agreement with all men, smiling indulgently upon every vanity and betrayal. Be-cause this God is a God of Love, we must never differentiate between good and evil, for judgement partakes of uncharity and presumption. Because this God is a God of mercy, we must pretend that sins have not been committed, that evils under our own noses do not exist. Because this God is the Father Almighty, he will bless us abundantly if we do "the right thing"—and his blessing will be apparent in our cheerful coun-tenance, our unfailing good-humour, and our steadily increas-ing bank account. He only wants to help us; to lead us from earthly joy to joy, foot by foot up the steps of prosperity.

There is so much magnificent truth mixed up in this appal-ling falsehood that it smacks of perverseness even to attack its perversions. But if we try to change the face of eternal God, we indulge in the supreme idolatry, beside which perhaps, in the scale of sin, adultery weighs like a feather and murder like a farthing. Yet the sin is committed among us, within Christen-dom, within the Church—maybe within ourselves; for are we sure, after all, that we prayed to the true God this morning? The God whose face is the face of the living and dying Christ? Or was it this God who, in grand avuncular benevolence, slyly slips us half-a-crown and tells us to have a good time?

Let there be no mistake about it. This God of Sentimental

Theology is a likeable God. God knows, God himself knows, we like this God, we natural men, better than we like the Body crucified and the Head crowned. But then, when was Christianity likeable? Never, of course. For Christianity can only be likeable when nailed-out hands are coveted and human souls cry out for chastisement. Suspect the propaganda of likeable religion. Suspect the false prophet who, even in the name of the redeeming Christ, wants to put you in touch with an unfailingly indulgent God. Suspect that offer of a private telephone line to the Heavenly office, where sits the eternal Solver of all your problems, the Guarantor of all your human hopes and wishes.

The God of Christians, if he is truly revealed in Jesus Christ, is not a distributor of earthly success and prosperity. His chosen course on earth brought his disciples to a shameful rout, and the most faithful ones to the foot of his cross. Few of us have the right to declare what is the true nature of that Kingdom of Heaven in which we are called to share here and now. But many of us can safely say what it is not. It is not an eternal Speech Day, at which prizes are handed out to the week's best pray-er of prayers and the week's best doer of good works. God chooses no "Man of the Year" to whom to present a silver trophy—a cup flowing over with health and wealth. Nor does he select the ideal "Miss Christian 1957" to be lavishly entertained at his expense, and then to open bazaars in his name. If we turn earnestly to God, imagining that we are entering a discreet competition for the award of earthly well-being, then sooner or later, with more or less pain, God will make plain our error.

And now, I fear, the complaint will be raised that we are making of Christianity a religion of tragedy, perhaps even of despair. But we are not. Our main immediate aim is to put suffering where it belongs, near to the human heart, because it is near to the Divine Heart; at the centre of man's realizations, because it is there at the centre of God's. And suffering is not all sadness: still less is it despair. Are the invalids amongst our friends the least inclined to smile? Have we not sensed a deeper peace, even a deeper joy, on the bed of pain than on the bed of sloth or the bed of lust? This alone is sufficient to prove that a faith which embraces suffering is not necessarily a religion of sadness or tragedy.

It was perhaps never more necessary to say this; for we have in our midst to-day a new popular "religious" literature, represented in France by Mauriac and in England by Graham Greene, in which Christian doctrine broods darkly over human life in an atmosphere of preternatural gloom. The costliness of faith is frequently measured by the agonizing denial of human passion, chiefly sexual. Now there is no doubt that, as an antidote to the Sentimental Theology of the eternal-Bank-Holiday variety referred to above, this movement may serve a useful purpose up to a point. But this is a negative virtue only, and it is always dangerous to try to counter extreme by extreme, exaggeration by exaggeration. And the fundamental joylessness of much of this literature raises grave questions. Indeed it is disturbing—and not only to the Roman Catholic—that the Quaker writer Christopher Fry should be able to show the sacrificial cost of human love paid in laughter and bubbling self-release, while the Catholic writers Mauriac and Greene can only represent this cost in terms of lacerated hearts and lives deprived of light. We shall have more to say on this later.

That suffering and earthly failure are in the very centre of that pattern of divine activity given us in the incarnate life of our Lord—this is peculiarly relevant to us to-day because one of the diseases of our time is what is called "frustration". On all sides we hear the complaint that men and women are frustrated. It is worth-while, therefore, to spend a little time examining what is meant by this complaint and analysing the situation which has produced it. In order to simplify matters, we must restrict our attention only to complaints of frustration which are manifestly worthy of consideration. That is to say, we shall not waste time on the frustration of the thief who finds it difficult to operate successfully or who finds himself in gaol. Nor need we concern ourselves here with the alleged frustration of the big business magnate who is prevented by high taxation from buying a luxury yacht, or of the debauchee who finds the marriage bond a cramping obstacle to promiscuity. We shall merely consider the complaint of frustration from those who have good reason to believe themselves involved in laudable activities.

The complaint of frustration, which is worthy of respect, can only mean that a man finds himself totally impeded from realizing worth-while achievements upon which he has set his heart. It will do no good to conceal that many worthy men find themselves in exactly that situation to-day. Setting out with high ideals, perhaps in the sphere of politics, public service, education, or even in the Church, they reach a point at which they find all their best endeavours blocked. After long experience of persistent effort and subsequent failure, they vent their disgust upon "the system" within which they have to work, and their wrath upon the "powers that be" who direct that system. Perhaps they become cynical: perhaps they give themselves up, at the most potentially fruitful point of their careers, to cultivating their gardens, while merely going through the motions in their chosen avocation: perhaps they burst out in rebellion and ruin their careers. In any case, it is a great tragedy, and one which we have no right to paint less grave than it is. The spectacle of men of ideals and wisdom, gifted with great practical capacities, bound hand and foot from exercising their faculties to the benefit of their fellows, is one of the most pitiable spectacles of mid-twentieth-century civilization. Thus politicians find themselves fettered by the party system and the party leaders, public servants by red tape and insensitive direction from the top, teachers by administrative machinery and H.M.I.s, parish priests by parochial church councils and perhaps even by bishops. Many of the fettered are worthy men, and we know it: many of them much worthier than their superiors, and if we do not yet know that, our education for modern life has scarcely begun. Must we blame the "systems" or the "powers that be"? The answer to that is that even comparatively bad systems can be fruitfully operated by leaders of the right capacity and intention. And, in any case, if systems are bad, it is the business of those directing them to ensure that they are improved. We are left with an indictment of those who direct our affairs in the spheres I have mentioned, and in all other spheres in which worthy men find their worthiest efforts blocked.

Let us be clear from the start that this problem has always existed in our civilization—in all civilizations. The world would not be the World if the right men got into the right jobs. We hear frequently from the days of Shakespeare—that age of supposed optimism and fruitful expansion—the sombre groan at all the indignities "that patient merit of the unworthy takes". The problem is not therefore new. Is it then, perhaps, especially acute in our day?

We have reason to believe that it is, by virtue of certain historical "accidents". In the first place, as many students of the contemporary scene have pointed out, we must remember the massacre of promising young men during the First World War. These are precisely the men who ought now to be just retiring from posts of leadership in the spheres I have mentioned, after directing our affairs over the last ten or fifteen years. It would be folly to pretend that we have not missed them; that our society has not suffered from their absence. In the second place, the reorganization and rapid expansion of our systems at the end of the Second World War was a hurried development. It was not easy to find men for posts of responsibility and leader-ship. In the first flush of post-war optimism rash and hasty promotions were made in a desperate effort to get the machines working again. We are suffering now from the fruits of those rash and hasty promotions, and we shall suffer from them, directly and indirectly, for a very long time.

Recently public expression has been given to another reason for believing that we have not of late been well served by our leaders. It is a conjecture which one naturally hesitates to quote; but experience leaves one with no choice but to treat it with respect. The men who have for the past ten years been in charge of our affairs—in posts of leadership in our various systems and institutions—are quite naturally men in their fifties and sixties. These were the young men of the 1920s and 1930s, the men whom we, who were children then, learned to dis-tinguish so clearly from the older generation which had known the pre-1914 world. We heard two different voices in those days from the adult world; the voices of two generations in conflict.

The older generation of our seniors on the whole claimed to be Christians. They were sceptical about popular trends manifested during the 1920s and 1930s. They wanted, for in-stance, to go on training the young in religion, morality, ser-vice, duty, respect for tradition, and so on. But they were old in our eyes; and we put these oddities down to their years. They were old-fashioned, out-of-date. The younger generation of our seniors were quite a different kettle of fish. Whilst making due allowances for the limitations of such generalizations, we must admit that the young men we then looked up to were not in the least prepared to train their successors in religion, morality, service, duty, or respect for tradition. On the contrary, many of them seized every opportunity to debunk these things. For they were the generation that lapped up Richard Aldington and the early Aldous Huxley, H. G. Wells and Bernard Shaw. We must not blame them. They had their own teachers and prophets to blame: we shall lose ourselves in an infinite regress if we try to apportion blame. But these young men were devotees of those easy philosophies which have since been discredited—the doctrines of inevitable progress, of Rousseauesque naturalism, of freedom from discipline, dogma, convention, and tradition. They took Shaw seriously as a thinker; they even took Shelley seriously; they built up the sales of the *New Statesman and Nation*; they taught history as the progressive dethroning of tyrannies, literature and poetry as the sacred flowers of animal passion and abandonment; anthropology as the key to God-myths; and Freudian psychology as the explanation of all high aspiration and endeavour.

Intellectually they were a corrupted generation. Morally they were sentimental—caught in the misty dreams of a bogus romanticism which had lost touch with the human realities of pain, toil, and privation.

All this is too sweeping. Of course. But tone it down, qualify it as you will, the fact remains that it makes a valid point. And the men in their fifties and sixties who now direct our affairs belong to this peculiarly misled generation.

We work within bad systems, in bad institutions, under the wrong superiors. The Church itself, in so far as it is a human institution, suffers from the corruption inherent in all manmade systems. Thus, in one more direction, the individual finds himself involved in that pattern of experience which we defined in Chapter I. Setting out with high ideals, determined to give of his best in his chosen avocation, he comes gradually to the knowledge that possibilities which he had confined to the very fringe of his realizations, belong in the dead centre. The possibilities I refer to are: that the men who have authority may be unfit to wield it; that those who have power may have been corrupted by the very gift and exercise of power; that those who lead will put vanity and self-interest before justice and integrity; that the ambitious will pander to bad superiors and flatter their very weaknesses; that those who rule will put prestige and popularity before principle and loyalty.

Does this sound shocking? It ought to do so. Does it sound outrageously false? It ought not to do so: not, at least, to the Christian; for it is only a practical illustration of the truth of the doctrine of Original Sin; only a reluctant admission that we are up against the World, as well as the Flesh and the Devil. We ought not to be too surprised that this is so. When the time comes at which we must truly and personally face up to the world's rottenness, we are indeed brought, whether we admit it or not, to the threshold of faith. For experience leaves us with only two alternatives. Either we must escape from real contact with life into cynicism, sloth, neglect, or day-dreaming. Or else we must bring into the very centre of our realizations the fact that the world is the World, corrupt and corrupting: we must embrace the realization, grip it, scrutinize it, make it fully our own and fully meaningful. For if it is not made fully our own, we deny the evidence of our own experience; and if it is not made meaningful, life itself is rendered meaningless at the centre, where effort and aspiration are born.

Experience of the world's rottenness, and our own consequent frustration, these realizations can be made meaningful only in the light of the Christian Faith. Our Lord's incarnate life culminates in the supreme hostile encounter with the world's rottenness. We are not dealing with a God who is inexperienced in the ways of the world. We Christians have no knowledge of an incarnate God who achieved "recognition" and climbed the ladders of social advancement and professional preferment. God himself, if it is fitting to say so, has had no incarnate experience of a world where virtue is rewarded, effort successful, and integrity respected.

Whither is all this leading? Are we to pronounce a sweeping, righteous judgement upon the world we dwell in? On the contrary, our Faith teaches us otherwise. We are to enter into it at the heart and take its guilt upon us. Our Lord entered into it and took its whole guilt upon himself, because he had no share in it. We must enter into it and take its guilt upon ourselves because its guilt is ours.

Where are the words to express this adequately—this need for the Christian to come to grips, not only with sins, but with sinfulness? There is a difference. The virtuous man admits his sins. The Christians admits his sinfulness. There is a great difference. The boundaries of my sins are fixed by the range of my private conduct during my span of life on earth. But my sinfulness: that is a different matter. Its tentacles reach out to involve me in every hostility, sneer, or oppression I encounter, in every corruption that stultifies work in my particular sphere, that breeds war, faction, and frustration in this my century; in the same self-centredness and worldliness that crucified our Lord two thousand years ago.

The danger of recognizing our sins and not our sinfulness comes precisely at the point where we fully encounter the world's rottenness. It was upon us a few moments ago when we passed judgement on our contemporary leaders and indicted a generation. The danger is that we shall judge when we ought to repent, condemn when we ought to cry for mercy; that we shall pose as gods in a wicked world, feeding on the forbidden fruit that turns our very discernment into rebellion and damnation. For recognizing our individual sins will not of itself enable us to embrace and make meaningful the fact of corruption in the world we work in. We need to realize our sinfulness too—our inescapable involvement in the total guilt of a humanity whose organized systems corrode idealism and stultify aspiration, whose respectable authorities slaughtered martyrs and murdered God.

The world's rottenness is my own individual rottenness writ large. It is my own in the sense that, by my sinfulness and selfishness, I have contributed to the total human corruption which causes systems and societies to operate in the service of selfish men rather than in the service of God. I must not measure my own contribution to this rottenness against the contribution of others: for indeed the size of my own contribution has been partly determined perhaps by circumstances of heredity and environment over which I have no control. God alone can measure guilt. But if I see human selfishness produce a famine or a war, I am blind indeed if I do not see my own individual selfishness inextricably entangled in this wholesale rebellion of the human will. Let us put this in another way, for it is a crucial point. Fundamentally there is only one sin— the rebellion of the human will against the Will of God. In so far as my own will is rebellious, it is in tune with every act of murder, rape, or oppression committed this day in the world. My private acts of selfishness committed to-day, trivial though they may seem to me, nevertheless range me at the side of those whose more sensational deeds of cruelty or lust publicly advertise the rebellion of the human will. They bring me into a deep sympathetic alliance with the murderer, the swindler, and the debauchee. I too, like them, am in rebellion. I too, like them, am serving the self; a little more cautiously and subtly perhaps, being rather more sensitive than they to the earthly cost of extravagance in these matters; but what heed does God pay to that added touch of worldly caution and subtlety? He looks down to-day upon a human race engaged in obedience or disobedience. Be sure that he does not draw quite so fine a distinction between kinds and degrees of disobedience as we ourselves, to our false comfort, perhaps to our eternal damnation, draw.

What, then, must be my answer to the spectacle of the world's rottenness? I must desert the human rebellion which this rottenness represents. I must put at the service of God the only thing which I am in a position to offer—myself. I must do so, not only confessing my sins, but also confessing my sinfulness; not only as a man who has committed this particular sin and that, but as a man involved by these very selfishnesses in allegiance to that wholesale human rebellion from which I myself have suffered. Are we beginning to see the light now? This man's vanity and injustice have prevented me from doing good work to-day. But my own self-will is in league, indissolubly in league, with this, my enemy's, self-will. In attacking my own self-will, I weaken the human rebellion in which he is taking part. And I attack my own self-will by offering myself to God. The very force which frustrates me externally is in part my own wickedness; for, unobtrusively perhaps but nevertheless effectively, I have sinned my way into the mass movement of men against God. I have sinned my way into the movement which blights endeavour—even my own, which corrodes idealism—even my own, which blocks the working out of grace in men—even in me.

I must offer myself to God, then, bringing the burden of my sins and my sinfulness. I must ask that I may be cleansed and used. This is the only contribution I can make and, paradoxically, it is not strictly a contribution at all: it is a mere withholding of refusal. I do not initiate in my self-offering: I merely desist from rebellion. There is nothing redemptive about my self-offering. Redemption has been achieved, once and for all. But my self-offering opens the way for the flood of divine grace released by our Lord's atonement. The only truly positive act I can do is the seemingly negative act of deserting the human rebellion.

This is the Christian way, the only Christian way, though you as you read, and I as I write, we know that we are miles away from walking in it. Shall we say that it is not entirely our fault? That we were badly instructed in youth; that our teachers taught us only of the Sentimental God and not of the God with the face of the suffering Christ? Shall we blame others for our long ignorance of the way? We cannot do so.

We have already shifted the ground from under our feet. We have already seen the corruption of others—even the corruption of the Church—as our own corruption. Every sin we ever committed involves us in that rebellious movement which has tried to change the face of God. We are left with no one to judge, no one to condemn, except ourselves.

And yet, we wonder. Is there a time for judging the world's rottenness, as well as a time for judging our own? Perhaps. But to condemn what we cannot conceivably remedy is a waste of time. And the only evil we can fully remedy is our own personal rebelliousness. Yet if gloating upon the world's rottenness awakens us to the enormity of our own sins and our own sinfulness, by all means let us gloat.

There is a corollary to all this, this concern—"obsession" if you like—with the connection between our private sinfulness and the evils that poison our world. It is a heartening, gladdening corollary; dangerous, perhaps, if dwelt on too much, but needful as a source of joy and an inspiration to Christian purposiveness. It is this. Good is not unlike evil in the ramifications of its entanglements. If my private acts of rebellion league me with all the perpetrators of human wickedness, and even with the diabolical powers of darkness, so too my little acts of obedience league me with the great human movements of the Spirit and even with the incarnate God himself.

We must not forget this interconnectedness of all that operates upon this earth in obedience to the Will of God. Our little private acts of obedience to-day link us with that vast movement of the Spirit which is, even now, sending monks to their offices in communities rich in the life of worship and sacrifice, vital in the life of service and discipline. And that same mighty movement of the Spirit is, as you read, sending missionaries, doctors, and nurses out on works of mercy and evangelism in dark and difficult corners of the earth. Our little acts of obedience, our impulses of silent self-offering, link us indissolubly with the whole movement of human obedience to God, wherever and however it operates. Wherever there is worship, discipline, faithful witness, toilsome service, there is something in which our self-offering is involved.

Let us see it like that; and then we can forget the arguments which have produced this conclusion. That from the human race to-day goes up one mighty prayer of praise, embodying every single act of obedience to the Divine Will which men are granted to perform this day. And from this same human race to-day rises one tremendous shout of defiance against the loving rule of God; a shout which gives voice to every single act of disobedience committed to-day by the rebellious human will. At every moment, and in every act or thought, we swell the volume of that hymn of praise, or else of that cry of blasphemous rebellion. For, let us not deceive ourselves, there is no third alternative, no discreet maintaining of silence between the praising and the blaspheming throngs. In every act we praise or we blaspheme.

God acts upon earth. He acts among men and within man. He acts in self-offering. This is the pattern of divine activity revealed in the incarnate life of our Lord. This is God's way with men. In acknowledging it, we recognize the nature of the revealed God, the only God we know, the only God there is to know. To fit ourselves into this pattern is the way of the Christian. As natural men, planted in the life of time, we would gladly have it otherwise. Hence we invent the Sentimental God, who teaches rather than acts, who rules at a convenient distance, and who distributes rewards instead of disciplines. But, as children of the true God, we learn to rejoice in the privileges he has given us: the privilege of being, not instructed, but used by him; the privilege of being, not directed, but indwelt by him; the privilege of being, not the recipients of bribes and prizes, but the sharers in his own life of love and self-offering. The privilege of joy: and the privilege of suffering.

3

PERSONAL VOCATION

WE HAVE said that God is generally and ceaselessly —not occasionally and fitfully—operative in human affairs, in such a way that men are at all times either obeying him or disobeying him. This, of course, applies to voluntary actions only. Involuntary responses have no moral quality. At first sight it might appear to be easy to make this principle of God's concern in all that we do look so ridiculous as to be incredible. Does God care whether I walk to work this morning on the right-hand side of the road or on the left? Does God care whether I wind up my watch before going to bed? Does God care whether I wear my red tie or my blue tie to-day? Since the sceptic would certainly attack our case by introducing examples of this kind, it is desirable that we should deal with them.

In the first place, we must remind our critics that, if we use the word *God* at all, we inevitably refer to a person whose intelligence is not less than our own. That is axiomatic. It follows that issues which are trivial to us, on the basis of our best judgement, are probably trivial to him. If they are truly trivial, we may properly say that God would not wish us to concern ourselves seriously about them. That is to say, if there is nothing of any kind to be gained by walking on the right side of the road instead of on the left, or vice-versa, we may assume that God's will is that we should not treat the issue as of any moment at all. Where there is a case of alternatives which are perfectly balanced in this way, then it is certainly God's will that we should not exercise our minds and waste our time in gravely pondering it. Indeed God's will enters into this situation in precisely this way—with the command to study things which are worth study. Thus, to the question, "Shall I give the bus conductor this penny or that one?" the proper reply is, "You ought to have something better to think about."

But if there is some slight (probably indirect) advantage to be gained from the adoption of one of the alternatives, then God, being a rational God, has the same preference as the rational man. Thus, if a secretary asks her employer, "Shall I sit at this side of the table to type?" his reply might well be, "Yes, if it helps you to do your work better." And this is, of course, the nature of the true reply to such questions as, "Does God care whether I wind up my watch before going to bed?" The value of decisions in these trivial matters depends upon the larger endeavours to which they contribute. Thus, if I spend this evening playing bridge, either I am indulging in needful recreation which will make me all the fresher in my next job of work, or else I am wasting valuable time which I ought to be employing otherwise.

The sceptic's supposedly destructive examples, therefore, constitute a valid argument only if we assume God to be less intelligent than ourselves and completely lacking a sense of proportion. In so far as a question is a matter of indifference to God, it ought to be a matter of indifference to us. That being the case, we shall not ask it. Indeed our transgression of God's will may lie in the fact of our asking it. If I worry much about the choice of my tie for to-day, I am plainly guilty of the sin of vanity. God's will in these matters is the will of the good and wise man. In matters of taste, good taste should determine our choices—the best taste we are capable of, that is. It is clear, for instance, that in matters of artistry and craftsmanship God wills us to keep the highest ideals in view and to endeavour to fulfil them.

Since we believe God to be rational, it is difficult to think of hypothetical choices which would be of no moment to him. Wherever there is a moral issue, it is of concern to God that we should make the right choice. And moral issues are involved in all our voluntary acts, though the connection between act and moral principle may be an indirect one. Perhaps we are undecided whether to buy this £30 carpet or this £50 carpet. Plainly the question whether we can fitly at this moment spend money on a carpet at all raises a moral issue: for the way in which we use our resources, and more especially the proportion which we devote to charitable and unselfish purposes, is certainly of moral significance. And the difference between the expenditure of £30 and the expenditure of £50 will bear some moral significance in relation to the general pattern observed in the disposal of our money. Quite apart from this, the question of the relative quality and serviceability of the two carpets will indirectly have its moral aspect. For instance, it is not only rationally indefensible, it is morally indefensible to waste resources on worthless material and incidentally to support those who are engaged in dishonestly exploiting labour and public by the production and marketing of worthless articles.

Our belief that God is concerned in all that we do does not of course rest primarily on grounds like these. But to show how fully our daily affairs, trivial or momentous, are related to moral issues, is to prove that there is no *a priori* rational presupposition against the likelihood of God's ceaseless concern in our doings. If an argument is to be produced in refutation of this claim, it will have to take some other form than the familiar *reductio ad absurdum*.

Since God wills the pattern of our lives, it follows that within his great design he has a definite part for each one of us to play. The belief that this is so lies at the basis of the Christian doctrine of Vocation, a subject which, while it has been fully studied in relation to such special callings as those of the priest and the religious, has otherwise been unjustifiably neglected. It is plain that the two ideas, Providence and Vocation, are closely connected. Indeed they are both complementary and mutually dependent upon each other. The doctrine of Providence stresses the ceaseless and ubiquitous intrusion of God into human affairs. The doctrine of Vocation defines a prime mode of that intrusion. Providence cannot operate upon free human beings except by issuing some call to them. All that Divine Providence asks of us—that is our vocation.

It is permissible and convenient (though rather artificial nevertheless) to distinguish between general and special vocation. The general vocation of all Christians—indeed of all men and women—is the same. We are called to live as children of God, obeying his will in all things. But obedience to God's will must inevitably take many different forms. The wife's mode of obedience is not the same as the nun's; the farmer's is not the same as the priest's. By "special vocation", therefore, we designate God's call to a man to serve him in a particular sphere of activity.

No elaborate argument is needed to justify the Christian doctrine of vocation. It follows indisputably from two propositions. The first, that God is everywhere active in human affairs and his will operative at all times. The second, that he is a rational God, fully aware that the world needs farmers and miners as well as priests and nuns.

Quite apart from the matter of practical obedience by individual Christians, the doctrine of Vocation is important as a general theoretical guide in relation to vexed issues in modern life. This aspect of the doctrine of Vocation has been sadly overlooked. Consider, for instance, the question of gambling generally, or of Football Pools in particular. Many Christians who can find no sound moral arguments against gambling as such (when it can be "afforded", as we say) are nevertheless unhappy about it. They might do well to consider it against the background of the doctrine of Vocation. For instance, it is difficult to prove the Football Pool in itself any more open to condemnation on moral grounds than the parish raffle—difficult, that is, until we introduce the doctrine of Vocation. It is arguable that the possibility of fortuitously winning a massive fortune is in line with the fact that one man is born to poverty and another to wealth through no virtue or deficiency of his own. Again, this possibility may be said to put the possession of wealth in its right perspective, as itself a fortuitous and not very significant fact, totally unrelated to virtue or character. We may even claim that this possibility helps us to see money itself as it ought to be seen—a possession unfit to confer either worth-while status or covetable dignity. On the other hand, as soon as we bring the doctrine of Vocation into the argument, we are faced with a much graver and more formidable question. Is it conceivably in accordance with God's will that thousands of human beings should be employed in Football Pools? That for thousands of men and women the operation of this machinery should be a central purpose of their daily lives? Once that question is raised, the difference between commercial gambling and the parish raffle is clear; and comparisons between the two are seen to be irrelevant to the controversy.

There is no doubt that the wider application of the doctrine of Vocation in consideration of contemporary life would clarify Christian conviction, perhaps very uncomfortably, in many directions. Matters might well be brought under Christian judgement which would otherwise be overlooked or regarded with discreet connivance. Consider the growth of advertising, publicity, and cheap journalism. Or consider the increasing multiplication of various kinds of unnecessary administrative mechanisms in connection with government and the public services. These developments would, under examination by reference to the doctrine of Vocation, prove to have a grave moral as well as an economic aspect. Advertising provides a useful example for our purposes. In noting the damage that advertising can do to those who come under its influence, we have neglected the damage done to those whose main purpose in life is to conceive, execute, and propagate it. We have condemned the advertiser's appeal to passion and appetite. Some have condemned the waste of resources which advertising represents. Must we not also condemn the spiritual exploitation represented by the employment of human labour and talent to such an unworthy end?

This evil of spiritual exploitation is an urgent matter in our age. Moralists tend to be behind the times in their judgements upon society; and there is no doubt that the evil of spiritual exploitation has now replaced the evil of economic exploitation in the lives of our contemporaries. Spiritual exploitation is the use of human labour and human talents in the service of an end utterly unworthy of them. For instance, what unworthy exploitation of hand and brain, literary skill, artistic skill, and craftsmanship goes to the production of the vulgar Sunday paper or the vulgar weekly. And we must not think that this evil is confined to the world of commerce. It interpenetrates all our modern institutions on an unprecedented scale. Consider the passion for recording on paper to no end at all—a passion in whose service hundreds and thousands of administrative clerks spend all their working hours. Or consider the meaningless statistical researches by which university sociologists and others deceive themselves that they are involved in the life of learning and therefore, presumably, in the pursuit of truth.

Is there no issue for the Christian conscience here, if our civilization is virtually denying to millions of souls the very possibility of fulfilling a divine vocation in the dominant activity of their days? Vocation is the voice of Providence, and Providence is always purposeful. Christians have never had any difficulty in showing that drudgery can be divine—if it is purposeful drudgery. Rooms have to be swept and roads too. But what are we to make of activities which our best judgement declares to be meaningless? We have been too neglectful of this issue, as perhaps can best be shown by a pertinent illustration. When I wrote an imaginative account of Hell,[1] I pictured a university in which brain power was expended in making meaningless statistical surveys of supposed human qualities like the *Disposition to Social Adjustment, Functional Initiative,* and *Innate Gumption.* A reviewer in a religious journal complained that activities of this kind were unpleasant, but *surely not evil.* In reply it must be insisted that any theory of Providence and Vocation will necessarily involve grave condemnation of the exploitation of human capacities to an unworthy, because meaningless, end. A picture of Hell riddled with economic exploitation of the under-privileged would have raised no religious eyebrows: but, as a critical commentary on twentieth-century British civilization, it would have been grossly out of date. We are no longer up against economic exploitation as the old socialists and reformers understood it. We are up against spiritual exploitation—the large-scale application of human faculties, manual and intellectual, to fundamentally purposeless ends.

The very topsy-turviness of our society makes of this a crucial personal problem for many people. There probably was never before in history a period when so many of the "most important" positions in civilized society represented the least fruitful functions. The point comes for many a man at which he is invited, in his chosen calling, to step into the back room. This involves forsaking work which is patently useful for activity which is patently useless. The man who is consciously serving his fellows and the community is asked to accept promotion to a post in which he will be occupied in recording or estimating

[1] *Cold War in Hell* (Longmans).

how other men are serving the community. The man who is doing a purposeful, practical job is raised to a new level at which he manipulates bits of paper and telephone receivers. Too many gifted men are lifted out of the stream of life in which they influence people and events, to become for the rest of their days the writers down of material which no one will ever read.

This system reason condemns. But the condemnation of reason is not enough: it is too powerless when the individual is faced with an attractive increase in salary. A moral judgement is called for: and the Christian doctrine of Vocation will provide it. No man with a true sense of vocation will allow himself to be promoted from useful to useless work. But vocation is the only power that can impede this evil of spiritual exploitation, which now corrupts our society on so large a scale. Especially among Christians we need a new race of men who will refuse to leave active spheres of life for the sterile and moribund business of sending out forms and initialling scraps of paper.

There has probably been too much sentimentality in religious teaching about work. We talk airily about the dignity of work, for instance. Now dignity is a fine thing in its proper place, but it is frequently quite out of place when a job of work has to be done. The first thing a man must put aside, if he is bent on cleaning out a sewer, or grappling with a burst water pipe above the lavatory cistern, is his dignity. It is an insult to the human species to suggest that the dignity proper to man is notably expressed in occupations of this kind. Of course, the reply will be that we don't mean *dignity* when we talk of the "dignity" of labour. We mean that labour is worth-while. Which is exactly the point made here: that work is, or ought to be, worth-while. It ought to serve a purpose.

As Christians, no doctrine compels us to believe that work is necessarily either dignified or pleasant. Indeed we are told that it is the curse of fallen man. But as Christians, convinced that life is purposeful, we must necessarily believe that human toil should serve a worthy end. This is our criterion in judging human activities. And, of course, this criterion enables us to justify the cleaning out of sewers more convincingly than we can justify the filling up of forms, the compilation of statistical tables, or the composition of a gossip column for the daily press.

Twenty years ago, when the major social evil in our country was the existence of mass poverty and unemployment, it was the duty of Christian teachers and writers to judge this evil in the name of Charity. But economic exploitation of the under-privileged is no longer a significant social evil in our country. The cry that went up in the inter-war period—Life is cruel and unjust—has been replaced by a new cry—Life is meaningless. Now the Christian apologist did not answer the inter-war cry by denying that life was cruel and unjust: he stressed that it ought not to be. And, if life has been rendered meaningless for many of our generation, it is not our business to deny their complaint, but to analyse the situation which has produced it, and to show that life ought to be other than it is.

If indeed we have merely substituted spiritual exploitation for economic exploitation, we have not perhaps improved matters greatly. It may be doubted whether the imposition of physical hardship and privation does more damage to the vic-tims than their enforced subjection to a pattern of life which is patently purposeless. Be that as it may, we are faced with a social problem which cannot this time be tackled in the name of Christian Charity: it must be dealt with under the Christian doctrine of Vocation.

To clear our minds, let us examine the fundamental nature of social evils which assume this prevailing impersonal charac-ter. When we say that man is the child of God, we mean that that is the rôle he ought to fill, not by any means that he does in fact properly fill it. When we say that God acts ceaselessly in human affairs, we do not deny the possibility that men will be so corrupted as to pervert God's good purposes in their every thought and deed. The wholesale and final perversion of God's good purposes is the condition we know as Hell. Man certainly has the freedom to model his earthly civilization on the pattern of Hell. Thus, in so far as human civilization is so ordered as to produce acute poverty and economic injustice, it represents a perversion of God's good purposes and, as we say, a building of Hell on earth. In the same way, in so far as human civilization is so ordered as to involve millions of human beings in purposeless work, that too represents a perversion of God's good purposes and a building of Hell on earth. To build a society whose impersonal operations are a defiance of Christian charity is diabolical. Such a society provokes from its victims the cry that life does not proceed under the dominion of a just and loving God. They are right. It does not. Human rebelliousness has seen to it that it shall not. God's purposes have *to that extent* been thwarted. To build a society whose impersonal operations are a defiance of the Christian doctrine of Vocation is likewise diabolical. Such a society provokes from its victims the cry that life is meaningless and plainly does not proceed under the dominion of an active, purposeful God. Again, they are right. It does not. Human rebelliousness has ensured that it shall not. God's purposes have *to that extent* been thwarted.

In this sense, if our contemporaries cry aloud that life is meaningless and that they see no evidence of a purposeful God in control of the universe, this cry is an indictment of our civilization. It may indeed spring from a deep religious sense— a deeply offended religious sense. Faced with this complaint, it is not our duty to try to prove that meaningful which is in fact meaningless. Our duty is to show how life can and ought to be rendered meaningful.

The human mind builds its generalizations on the basis of particular experiences. The simple unlettered mind constructs its total vision of the shape of things by directly enlarging its immediate picture of the local environment. If day-to-day labour serves no other end than the maintenance of some meaningless administrative machinery or the production or marketing of worthless and even unwanted articles, it is difficult to see how it can provide a basis for a general judgement upon life as being purposeful and divinely guided.

The intrusion of the meaningless into life always represents the entry of the diabolical, just as the intrusion of purpose represents the activity of God. In that sense, meaningless labour must always be to some extent damaging to the human spirit. Fortunately, of course, this damage is partially offset by the fact that a man may do intrinsically meaningless work for the very good reason (in itself) that it enables him to support his wife and children. This means that the evils we are investigating are powerless totally to corrupt faith by destroying the sense of vocation in obedient Christians. Nevertheless they do damage by relating activity to immediate ends which are worthless.

This issue is seen in its extreme form when we consider the fate of men whose daily lives are spent in checking Pools coupons, in designing or distributing vouchers for washing detergents, in collecting scandalous copy for Sunday papers, in manufacturing useless plastic knick-knacks to catch the eye on the stalls of chain-stores, or in copying things down in triplicate in government offices. It is seen again in the development of what we call restrictive practices in industry. When the management of an industrial undertaking, originally built up to supply the public with certain commodities, operates towards the curtailment of supplies of that commodity, then true purposefulness has been perverted. When a trade union, originally established to safeguard the economic position of the worker, operates towards the disruption of the national economy, in the interests of little more than a technical quibble about whose duty it is to drill holes in sheets of metal, then true purposefulness has been perverted. These examples illustrate the prevailing corruption of meaninglessness on a large scale. But the issue touches millions of others more fitfully and occasionally in the course of their pursuits. How many of us have felt twinges of conscience when setting out on long journeys at the tax-payer's expense in order to attend meetings which serve no valid purpose at all? Here is an example which will perhaps bring home to many the widespread intrusion of the meaningless—and therefore of the diabolical—into contemporary civilized life. The fact that committees and organizational mechanisms proliferate rapidly every year testifies to the operation of evil in our midst in a novel and pernicious form. The fact that this evil especially and increasingly permeates public services established with the laudable aim of improving the nation's welfare, health, education, and amenities, is an object lesson in the Devil's power and ingenuity. But then our Faith has always taught us that it is the highest purposes which can be most evilly corrupted.

Of course this particular evil is absurd, and we are right to laugh at it. But we are wrong if our response involves nothing deeper and graver than laughter. For the problem of large-scale impersonal purposelessness in our systems, institutions, and national life, is simply the problem of personal frustration writ large. If we turn away from this evil with a smile, comforting ourselves that at least we have ironed out poverty and injustice in the Welfare State, we fall into the Devil's hands. By connivance and acquiescence we accept. And to accept the purposeless is to deny the power of Providence and the significance of personal vocation. It is a defiance of faith.

How can we make this crucial point most effectively—for it diagnoses, not the sickness of yesterday, but the sickness of to-day? Everything, everything in our national life, in our personal lives, which expresses the meaningless is a part of the gigantic pattern of our age's faithlessness. We are tempted to smile and nod at the purposelessness of so much contemporary activity, and then to return to our cosy little worlds of private self-indulgence. Or, if we are more reflective by temperament, we brood tragically on the absurdity of things and shrug our shoulders in despair. It is the tragedy of Hamlet. The tragedy of the meaningless, not embraced and resolved through the power of faith and self-surrender, but accepted and pondered as a madness at the heart of things.

A thousand wise voices have told us that the social evil of our day lies, not in economic injustice, but in administrative waste and purposelessness, in bureaucratic formalism and red tape, and in the stultifying dominion of form, regulation, and paper rule over positive purpose and effort. Another set of voices tells us that the dominant sickness of our time is, not the sickness of diseased body, but the sickness of the diseased mind, overcome with the sense of purposelessness, frustration, and despair. Yet another set of voices tells us that the prime evil of our day is the lack of religious faith. These three charges are true. But what we have as yet quite signally failed to understand, is that these three charges are one and the same. Each of them testifies to the intrusion of the meaningless into human life, either at the personal or at the impersonal level. If we continue to nurse and cultivate the purposeless in the organization of our impersonal affairs, we shall certainly feed the sense of purposelessness in our private careers and in our individual visions of life as a whole. It follows as the night follows the day. Certainly there is a dominant sickness of our day. It is the lack of faith. And this diagnosis brings a judgement, not only upon our personal weaknesses, but also upon the notable corruptions of our impersonal systems and organizations. There is a Christian judgement to be passed even upon the laughable paper form, the wasteful, time-filling job, the superfluous administrative mechanism. And it turns out to be fundamentally one and the same with the Christian judgement upon the widespread scourge of mental disease and neurosis. We have now indicated the general lines such a judgement must follow, and its necessary basis in the doctrine of Vocation.

Like all abstract nouns which denote aspects of God's dynamic activity, the word *vocation* tends to put into our minds a too static concept. We have seen earlier that the abstract noun *Incarnation* has the same tendency. The compilers of the creeds were wise indeed to frame the formal declarations of Christian belief by means of verbs. Not, *I believe in the Incarnation*—a phrase which certainly opens the way to misinterpretation— but, *he came down from heaven. And was made man*—phrases which in fact leave no room at all for doubt about what is meant. Again, we do not recite, *I believe in his Resurrection,* but, *the third day he rose again.* This is a point which deserves to be emphasized. Modernist diluters of the Faith rely upon subtle and highly abstract connotations of words like *Incarnation* and *Resurrection.* We do well to remind them that no degree of intellectual subtlety exercised in interpretation of these abstract nouns can affect one whit the clarity and directness of the credal propositions. *He was made man. The third day he rose again.*

These abstract nouns are useful. The history of theology is such that we cannot now do without them. Nevertheless it is conceivable that the history of Christendom might have been a happier story had they never been invented. Certainly they indirectly open doors to unbelief. We can get ourselves into a fine intellectual and spiritual tangle by chattering about the *divinity* and *humanity* of our Lord, so long as we chase nouns and avoid verbs. But there is not much we can say to tone down the force and vividness of the scriptural and credal statements. God was made man. The Word was made flesh.

It is necessary to say this because the noun *vocation* is merely a convenient form of reference to a process which is dynamic. We are called *to be used* by God. To forget this is to be in danger of simplifying and reducing God's claim upon us. As long as we think of our vocation as "a thing", it represents a demand which perhaps can be easily satisfied. If my vocation is simply to be a doctor, then God's demands are presumably satisfied when once I am qualified and start to practise. But, of course, my vocation is to be used by God throughout my whole life. It may be that I have good reason to believe it God's will that I should be used as a doctor. But there is no sense in which God's demand can be regarded as fully and finally satisfied at some point in my career.

Thus it is an over-simplification to polish off the theory of vocation by listing callings in which God uses men and women —as priests, doctors, nurses, teachers, farmers, and so on. God's willed use of me may involve my wanting to be a doctor and failing to become one. I may be used in a discipline of that "unsuccessful" kind. We have already seen that God can use failure. It may be the very thing he intends to use in my particular case.

My vocation, therefore, is not a limited demand which can be satisfied by my decision to work in a particular sphere. My vocation is to be used by God as he wills, and the pattern of this usage is quite unpredictable. Since we do not understand the relationship between the temporal and the eternal, we cannot even say whether God himself exactly predicts the pattern. Human beings are free. The circumstances in which I shall find myself living in a year's time will be determined by numerous yet unmade decisions on the part of free men and women. God will wish to use me in the situation which they in part create.

Now this way of putting it admittedly has its dangers. We must beware lest we picture ourselves as the elect, desperately needed by God for the fulfilment of his purposes when other men seem likely to thwart them. We are not going to be used by God in the sense that we shall help him. God does not need our help. We are going to be used in a given situation in the sense that God will enable us to glorify him through all the rigours of that situation, by being obedient and trustful in the appropriate mode.

We most of us set out on the Christian way with the idea that we are going to help God. We give ourselves to undertakings which we earnestly believe will benefit his cause on earth. In the early stages of the Christian life this is perhaps not a very culpable error. It is the beginner's mistake—the mistake of the child who has missed the point, rather than the proud assertion of self-will. But if we even begin to pray, as well as to work, we shall soon learn our error. For one of the first things that God teaches those who try to serve him is that they are not indispensable. Thus perhaps our undertaking fails —not completely or disastrously, we are not yet strong enough for that, that is a distinction reserved for his saints—but sufficiently to make us re-examine our motives and aims, and to bring home to us our error. For what was our error? That we pictured ourselves helping God, doing something for him of our own will and resources. As though we could contribute something which he had not first given us! Thus we learn that, in so far as anything worth-while was done through us, it was done by God. And indeed we learn this most crucial lesson: that in so far as our efforts have produced results fruitful for the life of his kingdom on earth, that is not something for which God's thanks are due to us, but something for which our thanks are due to God. We cannot, if we are discerning and obedient, fail to grasp this point. We see that what we have done or said has here and there brought light to another soul. But at the same time we see that the mode and circumstances in which this help or light was transmitted were in fact such that it could have been effected just as well by some other instrument than ourselves. Recognizing this, we realize immediately that, far from our having done something helpful for God in our work, what has happened is that God has done us the unmerited honour of choosing that particular work of ours as his instrument.

It has already been said in this book that, in praying daily to be delivered from evil, we are, most of us, praying that God will not give us great success in our undertakings. No doubt for most of us this same prayer is also a prayer against complete failure. It takes a strong soul to stand up to either. We have reason to thank God that, of his love and his mercy, he grants us that carefully calculated mixture of modest achievement and restrained disappointment by which he ensures that we are not tempted beyond our resources. We have also reason to pray for God's especial help both for those who achieve great successes and those who suffer bitter failures; for they are greatly tempted and, oddly enough, their trials are not dissimilar. The pride of achievement is not very different from the pride of despair.

Achievement and failure, both alike ought to bring us to our knees in prayer; the first in thankfulness for God's gift to us, and in sorrow for our own unworthiness; the second in admission of our humble dependence upon God, and in thankfulness that his will has been done. For of one thing we can be sure: if we pray about our undertakings, God's will certainly will be done, in some way, in and through them. And the wonder is—as experience will teach us a hundred times, if we let it—when we pray the wrong prayer (provided that we pray earnestly and sincerely) God will answer the right one.

Many a Christian prays for God's help in some seemingly crucial undertaking entered upon for the furtherance of his kingdom. His efforts are then totally, it seems, frustrated by the decisions and acts of other men, apparently misguided by error or influenced by selfish and worldly considerations. Does this mean that the prayer has been rejected? At first perhaps the individual is tempted to think so. But, if he continues to pray, he learns that opportunities have been given him for a kind of service quite different from that he originally pictured himself performing. This service, accepted and performed in the humility bred of disappointment, represents a degree of unselfish obedience which, as he now realizes, he would never have attained in the successful execution of what he originally planned. This new service is wholly of God's giving. He thanks God for it and realizes that, though the prayer he consciously prayed was the wrong prayer, God accepted his act of prayer and answered the right one.

Thus the Christian life is, in a very grave sense, a hand-to-mouth affair. The Christian embarks upon every worth-while undertaking with a prayer for God's blessing upon his endeavours, but expecting nothing definite. Expecting nothing definite in the way of earthly results, that is. Certainly he expects the blessing he has earnestly prayed for. It is a part of his faith that he should expect that blessing: but it is equally a part of his faith that he should expect it without any attempt to define or anticipate what form that blessing will take. Any attempt to define in advance what the precise nature of God's future action is likely to be is a weakness of faith and an expression of uncreaturely pride. It is not our business to assume the god in our plans and expectations for the future. When entering upon any undertaking, therefore, our prayer must be one of submission in advance to God's future fulfilment or rejection of our particular plans and efforts. We must pray that God will accept whatever is worthy in our motives and endeavours, and forgive whatever is unworthy; that he will use all we do *in his own way* for the furtherance of his good purposes and not ours; that he will give us the grace of obedience to his "future" decisions in the mode appropriate to those decisions; that he will save us equally from vanity in success and from despair in failure.

We cannot understand in advance what God's good purposes are in detail. To think and act as though we do understand them, in forwarding any undertaking, is to play at being God; for it is to step temporarily out of our true creaturely status of utter dependence and obedience. And here we touch upon a dominant sin of our age. We are all, to a greater or lesser degree, playing at being God. We live in the future, embarking upon schemes and ventures, not only because we know them to be right (which it is proper for us to do), but also because we clearly picture these results and those as the precise outcome of our endeavours. Of course we need to know where we are going, and to what ends we are working; but this general sense of purposiveness is something very different from the attitude which attempts to bind the future which only God can bind.

This attitude is with us in the religious sphere, and it mars much earnest effort which might otherwise be directly and fruitfully blessed. No man who has tried vainly in any sphere to influence thought and action in a worth-while, and even Christian, direction, can be unaware of what this means. One sets out to be a pioneer, and ends up perhaps by being a break-water. Or one embarks upon a crusade for furthering mighty ends which seem to represent God's own cause, only to find oneself eventually achieving nothing in that particular direction, but being apparently treated as a moral guinea-pig in an experiment which puts the maximum strain on charity and humility. We have the word of the saints for it that this is in fact frequently God's way with men. And it hurts our dignity. We set out on great tours to heal the soul of man, only to find ourselves at last patients in the universal spiritual hospital. Certainly it hurts. When a man sets out to break the world speed record for automobiles, and ends up by being gently taught how to ride a bicycle—and perhaps even being given fatherly encouragement for his first promise in the matter of keeping his balance—then indeed he is affronted. If he is fundamentally a wise and humble man, he is also, when he gets over the first shock, vastly amused.

God will certainly tickle our sense of humour, if we are not too proud to let him. He will make our pride and pomposity laughable in our own eyes. He will make us appreciate, not only the sinfulness, but also the sheer farcicality, of that self-reliance in which we embarked, self-initiating and self-propelled, to build the kingdom which he has already built. Of course it is amusing. We enter our names for the three-mile race. We train rigorously and scientifically. When the day of testing arrives, we don our running togs and put up our very best performance. And then, at the end of it all, we are sympathetically awarded a consolation prize for a very touching little effort in the Fancy Dress Parade. What eye-opening there is, and what irony! We thought—no, we *knew* we were good runners: we recognized where our real ability lay: we were gratefully aware of our outstanding talent in this one limited field. But, after all, it is not wanted. Our achievement is not applauded. Our performance raises no eyebrows. Instead we are given discreet and gentle encouragement for our worthy— if humble—little effort in a sphere for which we never had any talent, in which we never even wanted to compete. Indeed we were not even aware that our names had gone forward as candidates in that particular event. We had left that kind of thing to others. Was it not, after all, a little beneath our known capacities and skill?

So easy it is to choose the wrong vocation. Indeed, if we ourselves *choose* our vocation, it is almost certain to be the wrong one. For vocation is precisely what we do not choose for ourselves. It chooses us. It is God's choice for us. Is this, after all, so much out of tune with the general pattern of things? Most of us do not *choose* our wives. We none of us choose our children. Yet how right they are for us—especially when compared with so many things in our lives which we have actually chosen for ourselves.

God gives us our vocation: that is precisely what vocation is —the rôle God gives us. How does he reveal it to us? By making a particular course in life attractive beyond all other courses? Sometimes it is true that he does: and those whom he calls in this way are certainly peculiarly blessed. But more often, perhaps, it is the singularly attractive course which turns out, quite plainly, to be outside God's special call to us. How do we come to learn this? By experience, more or less painful; but only, of course, if we are living, to some extent at least, a life of prayer. Does this mean that God will speak plainly and directly to us in prayer? Rarely; or so we are given to understand by those whose ventures in prayer make them qualified to answer the question. On the contrary, God acts upon us as we have seen that he generally acts upon the human scene— among men, within man, and through the ordinary experiences of daily life.

We receive our vocation from God: but we do not receive it neatly tied up in a parcel. It is not a case of untying the string and removing the wrapper, and there God's purpose for us stands revealed. We have to pray hard and work hard to arrive at our vocation. It will not be delivered to us in the morning mail in a specially coloured envelope with a celestial post-mark. There will probably be no crisp, terse order that leaves us immediately free of doubt and uncertainty. God does not deal in telegrams. We must act that he may act in us. It is no good sitting about and waiting. We cannot turn on a radio and listen to the Voice of God. He does not sit with a microphone in his hand, ready to broadcast advice and instructions to those who tune in on the right wavelength. Our vocation is not something which, as we say, we can get hold of. On the contrary, it is something which will get hold of us.

84

PERSONAL VOCATION

This we can well understand, having seen in our Lord's Incarnation the pattern of God's way with men. He initiates and we respond. He sets the work afoot. He plans the drama. We fit in, or we do not fit in. The first thing our Lady knew of the Incarnation was that it was going to happen, and that she was going to be used in it. The first thing that men in general knew of the Incarnation was that it had already happened. God was among them, active at their side, speaking to them, asking to use them. He had come, and was at work. At first the rumour, the unrest, the questioning, and uncertainty: then the full knowledge. God is here at work among you.

So it will be in our own individual lives, if we are obedient. No clear signal at first, probably. Not a proclamation inaugurating the new life; but a disturbance, an unrest, and a subsequent period of questioning and uncertainty. That is the stage at which we must open ourselves to any eventuality God may bring about, the stage at which we must offer ourselves to God without reservations, hoping that he will clearly call and use us. Then the full realization. Not, probably, "God's plan for you is that you shall do this or this." No, rather, "God is at work within you already to this or that end. Allow him to use you fully."

We feel the demand before we know what is being demanded. God is the Creator: we are his creatures. Things do not pass between us as between equals. Thus we do not, strictly speaking, *receive* our vocation: we *discover* it. There is a great deal of difference between receiving and discovering. When we receive something, we accept it complete into our hands. But discovery is a gradual process. It is like digging up valuable remains. The excitement begins when we first learn that there is something there. Discovering exactly what it is takes time and patience—and a good deal of heavy spadework.

It is a useful analogy, because indeed we frequently guess wrongly in digging up our vocation. We think it is one thing, and it turns out to be another; usually something much bigger than we first expected. And yet it is a faulty analogy too; because vocation is discovered inside ourselves; and we cannot handle it, when we find it, like a Roman vase. On the contrary, it grows until it handles us.

Perhaps it is now becoming evident that the distinction between general and special vocation is a highly artificial one, which disappears when the subject is studied at all deeply. My vocation is to do God's will—and that plainly involves everything that God chooses for me. Of course it is theoretically possible for a man to say: I have accepted God's general call to me to be a Christian, but I have rejected his particular call that I should be a priest. Yet this statement will not stand up to analysis, since in so far as I reject any part of God's demand upon me, to that extent I am not fulfilling my vocation as a Christian. The Christian strives to live in obedience to God's will. Everything that God wills for him is part of his Christian vocation.

If distinctions must be made, it would perhaps be more helpful to distinguish between positive and negative vocations. This distinction at any rate has the merit of clarifying the true nature of the service we are asked to give. There is no doubt that God's action within men is sometimes manifested in positive achievement, and sometimes in the endurance of pain or frustration. All Christians, of course, taste both modes of service during the course of their discipleship, but in very variable proportions. Experience shows us that in some men the vocation to positive achievement is dominant; in others the vocation to endurance is dominant.

The Church is God's incarnate Body, and we must expect to see, in the life of the Church and in the lives of individual members, experience corresponding in some degree to our Lord's incarnate experience. The life of the Church in any generation will involve suffering as well as fruitful teaching and service. It is the frightening privilege of the Christian to live in Christ, and to share, in some measure, in the pattern of his incarnate career. And, if we may be excused for using an ugly word in this context, God seems to believe, as we say, in "specialization". Thus, though all Christians must come to know the way of the Cross, it is certain that some souls in particular are called to share more outstandingly in our Lord's suffering and "failure". There is the vocation to martyrdom—not only to martyrdom of the flesh, but also to martyrdom of earthly hopes and ambitions, worth-while in themselves. There is the vocation to prolonged physical suffering, which some saintly souls have indeed been able to accept joyfully and to offer thankfully to God, as something which unites them to the crucified Christ. There is a vocation, perhaps, to mental anguish—to a sensitive and tormented sympathy with those fellow men who suffer from pain, privation, and injustice; to an agonized and unappeasable indignation at the spectacle of the sufferings of the poor, the maladjusted, the deformed, and the down-trodden.

Is there a vocation to scepticism too? I do not mean a vocation to thoughtless or arrogant unbelief; but a vocation to unresolved doubt and questioning before the mystery of pain and loss, enacted on earth, as it so easily seems, under the closed lips and withdrawn hand of the Father. Is there, in short, a vocation to protest—not to rebellious protest (there can never be that), but to interrogative protest, deep, worried, passionate, before the spectacle of madness, deformity, and cruelty? A protest which almost (but not quite) cries shame upon God that he should remain hidden while such things are done?

We cannot doubt that there is a vocation to this—this dismay that trembles on the brink of rebellion, this bewilderment that hovers on the edge of faithlessness and despair. We cannot doubt that there is a vocation to the uttermost testing of faith and hope: for this too had a place in his self-offering. "My God, my God, why hast thou forsaken me?"

The cynic has a scoffing rejoinder at this point: "One more step in the argument, and you can prove that there is a vocation to sin." That is so often the Christian's position when he tries to speak of his faith. One more step in the argument, and you are lost in absurdity. It is a step which we must not take, of course. But, whilst stopping short of irrationality, we must yet go all the way that reason and experience will take us. And in this matter they both take us a good deal further than we really *want* to go.

For we have seen, some of us, a devout, saintly Christian, suddenly stricken with the total loss—not of faith—but of everything that makes faith joyful and vital, and perhaps even reasonable. Stripped of feeling, delight, fervour, and warm purposiveness in the exercise of Christian duties of prayer and praise, he is left clinging to a thread—the thread of plain, drab obedience, unilluminated by a single ray of hope or light or joy. God, it seems, tears from the heart every impulse of worship and thankfulness, every movement of living response to what is lovable and laudable, and leaves nothing but a numbed awareness that, through all the blackness of aridity, distraction, and unreason, the naked soul must somehow continue to say, "Thy will be done".

When we see this tragic spectacle—a man of valiant and selfless Christian service staggering under the weight of the world's faithlessness which he has never shared, are we too, the spectators, to say, "Thy will be done"? If we believe that to be our proper response, then indeed we have admitted that this burden too is a vocation.

Hitherto in this book the need has everywhere been stressed for Christians to deepen their awareness of God's activity among men and to awaken their sense of personal vocation. It may be well now, therefore, to mention some of the moral and spiritual dangers which especially beset people with a developed sense of Providence and vocation. In the first place, consciousness of God's unfailing purposiveness and of personal involvement in it, may easily breed a dangerous sense of being ranged in secret alliance with God against the majority of one's fellow men. When the Christian becomes daily aware of himself as God's instrument, he is tempted to see those who are ranged against him as agents of the Devil. Deeply conscious of his own rôle in the furtherance of God's good purposes, he cannot but feel that those who actively oppose the fulfilment of those purposes are themselves in rebellion against God. Because of this danger, we must never allow ourselves to forget either our own part in the human rebellion or the uncompromising demands of charity.

Moreover, in so far as the Christian is hourly aware of God's work afoot in the world, he is apt to exaggerate the number of God's foes. This is a very natural consequence. Any man who has become deeply conscious of the working out of God's purposes here below, will be especially sensitive to words and actions by which other men seem to confound the fulfilment of those purposes as the Christian understands them. He will thus see living evidence of rebellion against God on the part of men who, in the first place, have no picture of life as a conflict between the powers of light and the powers of darkness, and who, in the second place, even if they had this picture, would not be sensitive to their own hourly involvement in it. In this way it is all too easy for the committed Christian to nourish hostile and uncharitable feelings against men and women who are not in the least sensitive to the standards by which their activities are being judged.

The simple truth is that the committed Christian is not merely up against the pagan; he is (perhaps even more, to-day) up against the "Christian" whose Christianity has no relevance to anything outside the church doors except a few matters of personal morality. Thus the committed Christian, seeing the finger of God laid upon every activity he is involved in, seeing God's touch reaching out through major issue and subsidiary issue to the remotest recesses of action and decision, too readily perhaps identifies God's adversaries. For he sees hostility to the Faith expressed over matters which, to the average "Christian", do not touch the religious issue at all. This situation results naturally from that increasingly acute sense of good and evil which we have described as the inevitable concomitant of growing Christian obedience.

One consequence of this is that the committed Christian to-day frequently finds himself in a situation in which the claims of the Faith seem to clash with the claims of Charity. Loyalty to the Faith seems to demand a rigorous insistence upon a particular point of principle, policy, or practice. Charity towards those with whom he has to work seems to require the abandonment of this position, and even an admission that its abandonment is somehow a "more Christian" because "more charitable" course than sticking to it. Anyone who has been frequently subjected to dilemmas of this kind will know that apposite manuals of morality are badly needed in contemporary Christendom. It is presumably to this kind of situation that Kierkegaard's dictum peculiarly applies: With God man is always in the wrong. As a philosophical comment, this is both illuminating and disturbing. But to anyone in need of immediate practical guidance it is singularly unhelpful.

No pretence is made here of giving a complete answer to this question. But it is necessary to press the question nevertheless; for in the present situation in Christendom it seems inevitable that dilemmas of this kind will multiply rapidly—dilemmas in which Christian duties seem to clash, loyalty to the Faith and the claim of Christian charity presenting apparently opposite demands. These dilemmas necessarily arise when Christians of different denominations meet together for common purposes, and especially when they meet together to discuss or plan reunion. They arose acutely during the recent controversy over the status of the Church of South India ministry in relation to the Anglican Communion. They arise in the sphere of education, where it is alleged to be operating under the shelter of the Christian Faith. It is not possible for the Churchman to work in officially Church of England educational institutions without being aware of betrayals of the Faith which charity and respect for constituted authority seem to require him to acquiesce in.

Our doctrine of Vocation will help us to cope with these dangers, themselves the products of vocational sensitivity. One important need is for the Christian to nourish his awareness of *other people's vocations*. He must recognize the diversity of vocation, and what we have called God's policy of specialization. It is the grace of God, and not the power of the Devil, which makes the man of Franciscan temperament seemingly throw dogma and tradition to the winds in his pressing, ardent pursuit of the immediate charity, the immediate mercy, the immediate self-effacement. It is likewise, we must believe, the grace of God, and not the power of the Devil, which makes the ecclesiastical rigorist obdurate and uncompromising over matters of theoretical principle which would-be reformers tend to steam-roller through excess of ameliorative zeal.

Thus our doctrine of Vocation teaches us many kinds of patience. This is of great practical importance in the field of interdenominationalism. If we are still at the stage at which individual vocation makes men adamant in mutual conflict over issues raised by movements towards reunion, then quite plainly we are not yet at a fit stage to implement plans for reunion. We have to accept the fact that, in our sense of the words, God may not want reunion. If God's personal demand upon men in different denominations makes the continuance of denominational differences the only honest, God-inspired course, then it is plain that God is not immediately purposing reunion. It follows that we are playing at being God, if we push schemes in defiance of his expressed will. For we can be sure that, if God purposes immediate reunion, he can certainly produce the human situation in which it is realized without conscious defiance by anyone of his personal demand.

The same must be said of other dilemmas where Christian Faith and Charity seem to clash. If, while praying daily for God's blessing on your endeavours, you still find yourself repeatedly in situations in which duties conflict, you can only conclude that God wills exactly such situations for you. It is your vocation. Not a happy one, of course. But is the vocation of martyrdom a "happy" one? When have vocations been judged valid according to the degree of comfort they seem to produce? We cannot evade the conclusion that some Christians are called to bear the burden which we may well think Browning shrugs off too lightly in *Rabbi ben Ezra*:

> So, still within this life,
> Though lifted o'er its strife,
> Let me discern, compare, pronounce at last,
> "This rage was right i' the main,
> That acquiescence vain:
> The Future I may face now I have proved the Past."

Many who work in fields of supposed "Christian" endeavour, where every year the gap is revealed wider between the Faith of the saints and the codes of diluted twentieth-century "Christianity", may well doubt whether they will ever be in Rabbi ben Ezra's happy position, able to look back on their lives and pronounce for a certainty that this rage was right on the whole and that acquiescence worthless. It may well be their vocation never to know.

Another danger which besets those who are deeply conscious of their Christian vocation is the danger that they will develop a hypercritical attitude to the World. There is a sense, of course, in which we cannot be too critical of the World, but this is a very general, even abstract, sense, and we must be wary of its operations at the personal level. By an easy transference, hostility against "the World" may develop into hostility against those who hold positions of influence and eminence in the world. It is fatally easy to effect this transference, a transference to which many social reformers as well as Christian idealists are prone. We have already admitted that "the World" is topsy-turvy by the standards of Christian judgement. It needs no Solomon to teach us that getting on in the world is frequently achieved by the exercise of self-assertive tendencies in very dubious ways. We have all seen men of principle and conviction denied the full use of powers of judgement and direction by the world's fear of clarity and decision and its preference for vagueness and inertia. We have seen all too often honest work depreciated and flattery, vanity, and dishonesty rewarded. That is the way of the World.

We have also seen wise, upright men of true understanding, possessed of reforming zeal and imbued with Christian idealism, gradually undermined by this very spectacle of the world's rottenness. We have seen them gradually arrive at a settled state of mind marked by acute hostility to everyone who has gathered to himself office or prestige. We have seen—and indeed we can explain—their fixed assumption that everyone who gets on in the world is a conscienceless worldling. This automatic suspicion of the highly placed and the influential frequently develops thus in men of high intellectual calibre who have been disillusioned by experience. They become "characters", known for their acidity. They can be uncomfortable companions, because they never tire of overturning our complacencies. When told that So-and-So has just been given a place in the Honours List, a public office, a professorial chair, or even a bishopric, their first response is to ask by what particular iniquity this advancement has been obtained. And they are not joking. They mean it; mean it earnestly. Their experience, they believe, has taught them a just suspicion of every man who achieves success in the eyes of the world.

As with so many false or unbalanced attitudes, there is so much truth in this one that it is possible for a rational man to repose in it in complete assurance. Nevertheless we must condemn it as an offence against charity and humility, since, however sensitive we are to the evils of the world, we have no right to assume to ourselves the authority of judgement upon other people, especially upon those with whom we have no personal acquaintance. We know that God reserves to himself the right to judge our fellow beings. It is worth saying, however, that, spiritually dangerous as this attitude can be, it is probably less damaging in the modern world than the complacency against which it reacts. We need the jolt which these cynics give us; we need it badly to-day. For we must admit that a too ready alliance with the World has been the curse of English Christianity. It has too readily been assumed that a man in a position of some eminence in the world is likely to be the fittest to advise us on matters of morals and religion. The consequences of this assumption, and others of the same breed, have been disastrous for the Church. A diluted "Christianity", which committed Churchmen can scarcely recognize as having any connection with the Faith, has frequently been pressed upon us with all the force of a worldly authority irrelevant to the Church's mission and her claims. For instance, the most heretical and (in terms of the Faith) most uninformed sermons you can hear are preached in the chapels of schools and colleges, not by God's ordained priests, but by men who climb the pulpit steps by virtue of their position in the world of education. It is a tragic blunder to set aside for a single instance the Church's own discipline in this matter. We have need to recall the phrase repeated so eloquently by Roger Lloyd in *The Church of England in the Twentieth Century*, "Let the Church be the Church!" So long as we continue to make a false approximation between the Church and the World in spheres such as those of public life, education, and the armed forces, so long we shall continue to hand over idealistic and potentially active Christians to a wholesale disillusionment which sees the Church as hopelessly compromised with the evils corrupting our society.

The last danger besetting those who are deeply conscious of their Christian vocation is the danger of over-developing the sense of life's tragic quality. It is a bitter thing that the Christians most completely broken by the realization of life's tragic quality should be men acutely aware of God's activity among us and of their own personal involvement in it. Those committed Christians — clergy and laity — who in middle life collapse with mental breakdowns that bring them almost or actually beyond the bounds of sanity, are they not frequently men of great sensitivity to God's personal demand upon them? Are we not nowadays seeing this pattern repeated a little too often for our peace of mind? It has happened to devoted priests who have struggled single-handed in dirty industrial parishes, while yearly feeling more and more dismay at the betrayal of the Faith in situations where steadfastness is much easier and less costly than in their own.

This is an issue which generates heat. We have got to search our consciences about the demands we are now making upon our overworked parish clergy, and about the support we are giving or denying them. No publicized action or decision in favour of diluted, compromised Christianity is made in high places, or at comfortable seaside conferences, or in cosy

academic circles, that does not have its repercussions throughout the struggling, quivering Body which is our Lord's. Somewhere it strikes at the heart of a toiling parish priest whose
daily round of Eucharist, prayer, and ministry can be sustained
in peace of mind only if he is aware of his partnership in a
Church where betrayal is kept in check. The Church spokes-
man who sells the pass to the secular journalist, the exalted
ecclesiast who gives ground on the radio brains trust, the
notable and eminent layman who washes away centuries of
tradition in a few ill-chosen words at a mass-meeting, and the
Church journalist who writes of the most sacred things with
one eye on Fleet Street—each and all of these men numb the
sensitive nerves of the far-off parish priest whose day has been
spent with the impenitent sick, the hardened sinner, and the
glib young rebel against the fullness of the faith.

It is an immediate tragedy this, that cries out for remedy.
Never were faithful priests struggling more heroically, often
with a sense of spiritual and intellectual isolation, in their drab
industrial surroundings. Never too were public pronouncements, thoughtless or thoughtful, so widely disseminated to
ear and eye. The learned and eminent Churchman, priest or
layman, speaks a few compromising words, perhaps trying to
guard himself against indiscretion (never a very sure basis for
the utterance of the truth), and a quarter of the country's popu-
lation hears them. They hear them and repeat them, and in a
hundred parishes, with their struggling priests, the bottom is
knocked out of some patient work of instruction and ministry.

We have got to remember that, if the sense of life's tragedy
proves too much for a single overworked parish priest, we all
share alike both in the tragedy and in the blame. And we bear
an especially heavy load of blame if we belong to that noisy
and more or less eminent few whose chief hobby it is to issue
public pronouncements designed to make the Faith more

acceptable to "the World" and themselves more excusable (intellectually) for having embraced it, even in their eminence.

Of course our sense of life's tragedy, and the burden of doing apparently unfruitful Christian work, ought not to overwhelm us. But for some of us it is easier to guard against that than for others. And it is no doubt hardest of all for those who carry on the daily duties of worship, teaching, and ministry in uncongenial surroundings, whilst being made continually aware of betrayal from within.

The temptations of the tragic view beset most of us to some extent. A deep sense of personal vocation and of daily involvement in a pattern woven by the hand of God himself easily makes reflective Christians suspicious of the breeziness and buoyancy of the hearty Christians whose temperaments so ill assort with their own. Yet it is wrong to be offended by cheerfulness, which in itself must surely rank as a virtue. And perhaps truly and deeply joyful Christians were never more needed than now when, as we have already said, even our "Christian" literature suffers from the gloom of the currently fashionable tragedians. Perhaps the revulsion against heartiness is the first step in progress towards that undiluted sense of tragedy which rocks even some of our devoutest from mental stability.

Here, of course, is no intention to plead for a return to breezy, slap-on-the-back evangelism, or to blind optimism of the All's-right-with-the-world variety. We have had too much of it: and it has done us no good. To anyone who, in spheres of Christian endeavour, has been subjected to the potent and furtive tyranny of the perpetual grin, the smile of unlimited tolerance and non-committal is a dreadful thing. But it is not that kind of cheerfulness that we need to offset the sense of life's tragedy. Indeed familiar acquaintance with that particular brand of cheerfulness is a sure recipe for deepening the sense of life's tragedy. Rather we need the deep, unheard laugh. The laugh which is the measure of our own littleness and even of the littleness of our world: the laugh which bespeaks a sense of proportion grounded beyond the limits of our temporal span: the laugh which is thrown, not in the face of the struggling idealist or the rigorous dogmatist, but in the face of the fallen angel, corrupter of mankind.

4

OBEDIENCE AND JOY

THE READER may now protest that the accounts of Christian experience given in this book do not bear witness to Christianity as a religion of joy. Much has been said of human experiences in which divine demands are made that cannot conceivably be met in a spirit of bubbling cheerfulness. Although we have here and there explicitly said that Christianity is not a religion of tragedy, we may be accused of having more generally and implicitly represented it as precisely that. For we have said a good deal about vocations to endurance, uncertainty, and privation which must inevitably involve sadness.

We must not pretend that there is no problem here. There is a grave and pressing one, a problem that touches many Christians to-day and may be an obstacle to perseverance in the faith, the problem of joylessness.

There are many among us who, in youth, have felt keenly the delight of life as a God-given blessing, who have consciously felt the light of the Divine Face brightening their ways as they responded gratefully to created blessings in the form of natural beauty, friendship, sexual love, or perhaps music, poetry, or art. Later in life, rendered wiser and humbler, as they think, by years of prayer and by the discipline of sorrow and privation, they look to their persistence in worship, sacrament, and meditation for a conscious joy in God's goodness and abundance comparable to their youthful delight in created things. They do not find it, except perhaps in rare, momentary flashes which, by their very fitfulness, seem to constitute both a sad reminder of what they have lost, and an ironical comment upon the "failure" of their religious practices to replace it.

We have no cause to deny the reality of this burden. Still less is it our business to lecture those who bear it. Christians are hearing of the bounding joy of the Resurrection and are reading of the unquenchable joy of the saints, and they are failing to find the light of this joy shining upon their own days, and this in spite of their loyalty to the Church and their persistence in good works. In failing to find it, they become not only depressed but burdened with a new sense of guilt: for they begin to question the sincerity and depth of their own faith on the grounds that it is not productive of joy and of that inner peace which passes understanding. These Christians can perhaps be rationally satisfied by being told that there are vocations to endurance and patience unilluminated by the constant radiance of joy; but this answer does not meet either their emotional need or their moral predicament. For they are still uncomfortably aware, from a hundred hymns and sermons, that the Gospel of the Resurrection is a religion of triumph and joy. Their experience does not square with this at all. They know that they are neither recipients nor vehicles of the joy released by the risen Christ, and they condemn themselves for it. And the very act of self-condemnation increases their disquiet. They spin round in a vicious circle of self-critical introspection. I am not happy: I ought to be: my faith must be weak: but the very fact that I notice this represents a degree of sinful self-concern: I ought not to think about it: I am lost in selfishness: I was happier before I took my religion so seriously, when I was given over to many sins which I have now conquered: my persistence in Christian faith and practice has made me more miserable: it must somehow have made me more self-centred: I am thus increasing in sinfulness: and if I give myself with new ardour to the fulfilment of religious obligations, it will be but the measure of my self-concern, so that my fundamental sinfulness will increase: and so on.

The problem of joylessness has been presented in high relief because it is a grave and present problem. We have earlier remarked that current Christian literature tends to be tragic and gloomy, and we cited the names of Mauriac and Graham Greene. And, with the notable exception of C. S. Lewis's *Surprised by Joy*, current records of Christian conversion and progress in the Christian life tend to be deficient in the note of joy. Indeed we may suspect that the impact made upon the reader by C. S. Lewis's autobiography is the impact of something rather alien and remote from the mood of our age, even from the religious mood. Do we not feel that there is something more characteristic of our contemporary religious mood in the harrowing self-exposures of Thomas Merton, and in T. S. Eliot's ruthless scrutiny of human motives and his terse analysis of bitter inner conflict?

This being the case, it is natural to ask whether there are historical reasons why the temper of mid-twentieth-century Christendom should be grave rather than ebullient. It would not be difficult to prove that there are. For instance, we are still living in the period of revolt against nineteenth-century liberal Protestantism. Now we are not directly concerned here with the errors of liberal Protestantism; we are concerned with the prevailing temper which they bred. A general and basic characteristic of liberal Protestantism was that it came to terms with the world—not, of course, with "the World", as represented by moral evils in society—but with the world as represented by current movements of thought and culture. By its depreciation of ecclesiastical tradition and discipline, liberal Protestantism aligned itself with contemporary individualism; by its ruthless subjection of the Scriptures to a scrutiny which all but ignored the intrusion of the Supernatural into the natural order, it gave its own expression to the prevailing spirit of scientific inquiry;

and by its doctrine of unlimited tolerance in the matter of individual spiritual and theological claims, it transferred to the domain of religion the growing fervour of democratic egalitarianism.

In these respects, then—and no doubt in many others—liberal Protestantism, as the nineteenth century turned into the twentieth, found itself in comfortable alliance with the mentality of its own age, sharing the humanistic confidence, the sense of mastery, and the individualistic spirit which marked contemporary movements of thought. Thus the liberal Protestant, however deep his religious experience, was in the happy position, truly happy, of being fundamentally in tune with his age. His religion allowed him to preserve the sense of being in league with the civilization in which he lived. Now nothing is more conducive to confidence, optimism, and daily cheerfulness than this sense of being in league with one's own civilization. Indeed the psychologists never tire of telling us that man's well-being depends upon a harmonious relationship between the individual and his environment. This is true if by "well-being" we mean easy cheerfulness and confidence, but of course the Christian means something else by the word.

In our own age the situation is quite different in this respect. Consider the major current movements in Christian thought. Without going into the merits or demerits of the outstanding theological emphases in contemporary Christendom, we can at least say for a certainty that they do not put the believer into any kind of alliance with the civilization he lives in. Thus the various fashionable brands of rigorous dogmatism—Thomist, Papalist, Fundamentalist, Barthian—all alike set the believer against the stream of the civilization in which he lives—set him, not only in opposition to its morals and values, but in opposition to its prevailing intellectual temper, which is still confidently humanistic and naturalistic. And the same may be said of existentialist and personalist theology.

OBEDIENCE AND JOY

We Christians are at loggerheads with our own age to a peculiarly acute degree. It has been so in history before, of course, and no doubt it will be so again. But it was not so for the majority of English Christians fifty or sixty years ago. It is ironical that, by and large, we should now find ourselves combating attitudes which the religious, as well as the secular, culture of our grandparents has bequeathed us. The attitudes I have in mind are: the rejection of dogma; the rebellion against authority; the suspicion of the supernatural; the exaltation of the individual; and the prejudice against everything which falls outside the scope of either scientific or historic description. Now each of these attitudes bespeaks a state of mind which has confidence in human achievement and in secular wisdom. But twentieth-century Christians have lost confidence in both. Each of these attitudes expresses a state of mind that has come to terms with progressive, humanistic civilization. But twentieth-century Christians, as current apologetic shows, are up in arms against the individualistic and materialistic philosophies which lie at the back of our social and technical progress.

The theological development, which we have exemplified in an extreme form by quoting the transition from liberalism to dogmatism, is only one side of the picture. If theology has been moving away from secular culture, it is even more the case that secular culture has been moving away from theology. Thus the rift between the Church and our civilization has been widening rapidly during the last fifty years. Of course, as we have repeated several times in this book, the Christian is always up against "the World". But to be up against "the World" is not by any means the same thing as being at loggerheads with one's civilization. To be in conflict with "the World" is to be at war with acquisitiveness, greed, dishonesty, and corruption, as manifested in a system dominated by the pursuit of wealth and ease to the exclusion of spiritual and cultural values. One may be in conflict with "the World" in this sense, and yet be in tune with those predominant movements of thought and culture which represent the flowering of civilization. Thus, though the Christian will always be in conflict with "the World", he will not always be at loggerheads with his civilization. That will depend on the extent to which the dominating intellectual and cultural tendencies of his day are in accord with Christian truth. In medieval Europe it is possible that Christians had even more cause than we have to-day to be in conflict with the contemporary world—in so far as its systems were more brutal and unjust than our own. But they had little cause to be at loggerheads with their civilization, for the predominant intellectual and cultural trends were in fact generally contained within a Christian synthesis. To a lesser extent, this is true of nineteenth-century England too. Quite apart from the liberal Protestant stream, there is a confidence and reposefulness about the work of the best nineteenth-century theologians—F. D. Maurice, for instance—which springs from the fact that, though they are of course critical of the contemporary world, they have the air of arguing by reference to standards and basic premises established and accepted in the dominant intellectual life of their time. To that extent they too are in league with their civilization. By contrast, the work of unbelieving thinkers, like Matthew Arnold and Samuel Butler, gives us the impression of restless misfits, vainly beating the air, and sadly failing to make contact with principles or axioms firmly established in the intellectual life of their day.

We must not deceive ourselves in this matter. The main streams of our secular culture and intellectual life, in the twentieth century, have flowed right out of the region within which Christian theologians argue and preach. The basic premises accepted by the dominant intellectual current of our day are naturalistic and humanistic, and leave little room for rational appeals based on those authorities to which the Christian apologist inevitably has recourse—Divine Revelation, spiritual experience, and inspired tradition. Thus, in England especially, we find ourselves increasingly at loggerheads with our civilization at a time when perhaps we have reason to be slightly less in conflict with the ways of the World. For, paradoxically, the World has become less cruel and unjust of late. It has ceased to exploit the under-privileged and to condemn millions of our countrymen to poverty and privation.

These developments have had their effect upon the temper of English Christianity. For Christians it is a stimulating and invigorating business to come to grips, practically or theoretically, with the moral and social corruptions of the World, more especially because the assault upon injustice, cruelty, and poverty always carries with it the official support of leading elements in our secular civilization. But it is neither stimulating nor invigorating to attack established modes of thought which have the backing of contemporary culture, with its vast intellectual power and authority. On the contrary, it is saddening, frustrating work. We all like to picture ourselves in the vanguard of social progress. But we cannot possibly relish espousing causes which the most respectable and influential intellectual circles of our time regard as absurd, and even as the refuge of the ignorant. If the present diagnosis of our situation is correct, that is our rôle as twentieth-century Christians in the post-Christian world.

These are some of the *internal* (theological and philosophical) developments which have flung twentieth-century Christians into opposition against the spirit of their own age. Our thesis is that the sense of being at loggerheads with the temper of our civilization has robbed our religious life of zest, buoyancy, and cheerfulness.

External changes have aggravated our situation in this respect. Whether justifiably or not on theological grounds, sixty years ago the Church of England, as an institution, stood in a more comfortable external relationship to the world of secular culture. We may take, as a notable example, the sphere of education. Sixty years ago a very high proportion of the most eminent posts in the universities and schools of England were held by men in Orders. This fact represented a metaphorical baptism of our culture. It naturally bred the vague assumption that there was a connection between the possession of religious zeal and the attainment of influence and authority in the world of culture. When assumptions of this kind, unanalysed though they are, float in the back of the mind, it is easy for religious faith and practice to be accompanied by a temper of confidence, buoyancy, and cheerfulness. For the Christian, in some spheres at least, the world was indeed his world. Of course it may be questioned whether English Christendom really benefited from this highly artificial alliance with the world of culture: but that is not the point. Certainly it provided the background for cheerful and unselfconscious Christian profession.

Again, even more important in this respect was the fact that, sixty years ago, the clergy had a social and economic status which has since been lost. Preferment in the Church represented a very distinctive ascent in both wealth and prestige. When all has been said about episcopal expenses, the fact remains that, sixty years ago, a bishop was a man of some substance. So too were the incumbents of many favoured parishes throughout the kingdom. Once more, we are not concerned with the rights or wrongs of this situation, but simply with the state of mind which it nourished. And of course this state of mind was again one of confidence and optimism in relation to the ordering of things here below. Here was another reason, unanalysed and undefined, yet operative in the back of the mind, why Christians should feel that the world was their world. It gave their Fathers in God status and substance. Through Christian zeal and godliness a man might rise to an exalted position in the world. That was the kind of world it was, a world with which their Church was on comfortable terms. We can be quite sure that the depression of status from which our clergy have suffered, and of course their financial losses, have left their mark on the temper of the Church. We have one more cogent reason for believing that the world is no longer our world: we can see with our eyes that it is not so: that the religious zeal and piety which we naturally associate with the clergy are qualities to be pursued at the cost of social status and economic security. That is the kind of world we live in, one which penalizes a vocation to the priesthood by imposing life-long privation. This is something which quietly nags at our peace of mind. What we ought to do about it will not be said here. Certainly we ought to do something. But for the most part we do nothing; and consequently we are ashamed. How indeed, with this spectacle of clerical privation before our eyes, can we re-associate buoyancy and joy with the practice of our Christian profession?

We have now said enough to show that there are clear historical reasons why the temper of mid-twentieth-century Christianity in England should be grave rather than ebullient. Others may extend further the list of historical and theological developments which have thus deepened the rift between the Church and secular culture—the establishment of divorce as a respectable expedient has certainly played its part, and perhaps too the more open condonation of promiscuity and homosexuality—but it would be difficult to dissent from our general conclusion, that the contemporary Christian is out of key with his own civilization to an acute degree. It will be noted, however, that in considering historical aspects of the problem of joylessness, no attempt has yet been made to give the Christian answer to the problem. That is intentional. The answer can be given only in reference to the spiritual aspect of the problem, to which we now turn.

To put the Christian's comparative joylessness into its contemporary worldly context, mentioning some of the historical factors which might lead us to expect the temper of Christendom to-day to be grave, is not of course to condone or justify joylessness. That we must never do. Hence our central difficulty still remains, illuminated perhaps, but not resolved—that Christians, practising their faith conscientiously as they think, find their lives unradiated by the joy of the Resurrection, and their religious observances untouched by that glow of delight and transport which so many devout saints, and even martyrs, have claimed as their major earthly consolation.

In pondering this problem, the mind turns to Charles Williams's history of the Holy Spirit in the Church, *The Descent of the Dove*. Williams argues that, in the history of Christendom, large-scale manifestations of evil, diabolically inspired, have been actively met by the Holy Spirit working in men. They have been met in such a way that mass-adventures in evil have been matched by corresponding movements of the Spirit, which have a compensating force. Thus the luxurious and licentious excesses of the later Roman Empire were immediately "answered" in the extreme and arduous asceticism of the Desert Fathers. In speaking thus of "compensating" movements of the Spirit, counterbalancing large-scale manifestations of evil, Williams is not of course attributing to these movements any redemptive power. He is merely exemplifying the mode in which the Holy Spirit operates in man, which appropriately bears some definable relation to currently predominant evils on the human scene.

It may well be that this theory of "compensation" can throw light on our immediate problem. Surely the predominant sins of our day are lawlessness and disobedience; not cruelty—our civilization has made us too humane for that; not lust or self-indulgence—our environment, compared to that of previous centuries, is more restrictive in these matters; probably not even covetousness—for our social organization has put restraints upon that too. No, the dominant sins are lawlessness and disobedience—the headstrong disregard of the divine creation of man and the divine ordering of the universe; the careless and arrogant failure to take into account that man's status on earth is that of a dependent creature, subject to the will of his Heavenly Father; the proud persistence in constructing a man-centred civilization, a man-centred culture and philosophy, all alike defiantly forgetful of man's allegiances outside time. All this we summed up in Chapter I in the analysis of our age's carefree disregard of man's dependent, creaturely status.

If this is a true diagnosis of our major spiritual disease, may it not be that the Holy Spirit acts among us to-day in some notably compensatory form? That he involves Christians in a discipline which, like the discipline of the Desert Fathers, bears a relationship of correspondence to the dominant contemporary evils? That he impels those in whom he lives to a special form of stringent obedience that somehow counterbalances the vast spiritual lawlessness of our age? These suggestions are framed as questions precisely because they are nothing more than suggestions. It is obvious that they can be nothing more. But surely it is not irrational, in view of what we have said of our age's lawlessness and disobedience, to suggest that to-day, in the life of the Church, there may be a special divine emphasis upon sheer obedience, shorn of emotional consolations, and perhaps even bereft of rational corroborations.

We are dealing with profound and mysterious issues here. We are on the fringe of matters of which we have no right to speak; on the brink of inquiring into the secret purposes of God which can never be known to man. But we may make this suggestion and yet, I think, stop short of presumption. For we have said that the touch of Providence is always purposeful, and any reasoning which leads to the discovery of true meaningfulness will strengthen our faith and weaken the bewilderment that breeds despair. One is led to this conclusion: any man who feels that the dryness of his religious experience imposes an almost intolerable demand upon his faith and perseverance, may have reason to believe that he is purposely involved in a movement of the Spirit having a peculiar and potent relationship to the evils permeating our civilization.

If we find, after earnest and humble attempts to open ourselves to the will of God, that our religious life remains drab and prosaic, unilluminated by radiance or joy, we have indeed reason to conclude that our special vocation is to a discipline of obedience comparatively unrelieved by joy or exultation. And if a considerable number of Christians to-day are compelled by experience sincerely pondered to conclude that such is their vocation, then we are indeed in the presence of a movement of the Spirit of the kind described above. Since the touch of God upon human affairs is always purposeful, we must regard any large-scale manifestation of vocations to dry obedience as itself purposeful and significant in the pattern of God's operations amongst us. It is logical to conclude that these vocations to unilluminated obedience represent a corrective to the spiritual lawlessness and disobedience of which our age is pre-eminently guilty.

By "corrective" what exactly do we mean? We cannot mean by the word that our obedience is redemptive. All we can say is that the word puts our obedience into its place in the pattern of God's good purposes being worked out in our own generation. Nevertheless, to say that our obedience is not redemptive does not mean that it is either inefficacious or fruitless. Indeed it may represent the most necessary, because the most appropriate, brand of witness in an age of lawlessness and disobedience. It may be precisely and exactly in keeping with God's good purposes that, when we are asked what satisfactions we get from our religious observances, we should be compelled to reply: None, in the way of emotional satisfactions; none, in the way of delight or transport; none, in the way of bubbling joy and untroubled confidence: only the single unpoetic conviction that, in this respect at least, we are behaving as God's obedient children.

There are some questions which, when they are posed with the utmost care and deliberation, prove to have answered themselves. There are some problems which, when they are expressed with the maximum lucidity, prove to have solved themselves. It is probable that we are dealing with just such a problem here. If we have proved that persistence in comparatively joyless Christian practices is a special vocation, with a definite place among God's good purposes for men, then we have also proved that such joylessness must be accepted—accepted thankfully as God's gift, and accepted appreciatively as being purposeful and therefore meaningful. But if joylessness is accepted thankfully and appreciatively—understood and embraced—it ceases to be joyless. By accepting dry religious experience, fully and consciously accepting it without protest or bewilderment, we deprive it of the power to distract, sadden, or disappoint us. There is no experience which can be regarded, at one and the same time, both as God's purposeful gift to us and as a thing to be regretted and lamented. Grateful acceptance of any apparently grievous or disquieting experience effects a transition in which grief and disquiet give place, not of course to transport or ebullience, but to calm satisfaction and peace. Only the saints can speak of this transition known most potently in relation to physical torment and mental anguish; but we can all discipline ourselves to experience it in relation to less arduous and terrifying disappointments and deprivations.

We who sit to-day in comfort and tranquillity, and probably in health of body and mind, we scarcely dare speak of what this transition can mean, and ought to mean, in the life of the sorely afflicted Christian. How shall we dare to give advice to those in pain and anguish, we who find a burden and a cross to disquiet us in an experience so easily born as that of dryness in our faith and worship? We cannot presume to press this lesson home upon those who fully taste the pains of mortality. Nevertheless the general truth must be stated; for it applies to the pinprick as well as to the cancer, to the disappointment over trivial rebuffs as well as to the crushing blow of bereavement or tragedy. All pains, sorrows, frustrations, and privations, however trivial, however great, can be accepted, embraced, and transmuted into occasions of gratitude and peace. Each and every taste of vexation, failure, and suffering can be offered humbly to God, because he is the crucified as well as the crowned.

We tremble in saying—or writing—this, for God has a disquieting habit of taking us at our word. Suppose, having said it, we were put to the test! We hastily brush the thought aside. After all, we only meant to advise ourselves about the endurance of minor distresses. If the logic of our argument has led us to make statements about the endurance of grievous suffering, then it has taken us further than we wanted—or want—to go. Of course. Logic is a truly disturbing force in religious thought. If we do not want to be made uncomfortable, we had better leave it alone, and content ourselves with sentimental tit-bits. "Never trouble trouble till trouble troubles you."

Unfortunately for us—unfortunately, that is, for us natural men, at home for quiet, slippered reading between dinner and the bed-time Ovaltine—unfortunately the Christian Faith does not deal in such cautious platitudes. We submit ourselves to its premisses and the canons of its reasoning, and we arrive at—no, we are driven to—conclusions such as this one. That we must *try* (*try* safeguards us, I think: a prudent word, *try*) to face disappointment and pain as God-given occasions for gratitude. That, in the fulfilment of our religious obligations, we must try to accept the dry, the drab, and the disagreeable, and thus transmute it into the very ground-stuff of peace.

We have gone a very long way round in order to say a simple thing. It is the usual course of religious reasoning. We prefer the long way round, because we are thereby kept back a little longer from those ultimately inescapable truths which shake the hearts that seek them, before tranquillizing the souls that find them. This it is. We must look for joy only in the working-out of God's will, never in any pushing forward of our own. We can find joy only in partaking of the pattern of his good purposes. Do we see now what this really means? That we shall find joy only through our involvement in actions conceived by God and set on foot by God. Joy only through our participation in that which is initiated by God, worked out by God, and ended in God. Joy only in that which is begun, sustained, and finished beyond our world, beyond time, in Heaven itself. True joy, never in this thing, centred here, but only and always in that thing, the sign and seal of our eternal heavenly citizenship.

Once more our argument has taken us further than we wanted to go. We never meant it to come to that! We would gladly, we natural men, hoping that things will go well with our affairs to-morrow, we would gladly have it otherwise. But God has netted us again in the toils of his ruthless logic, and he allows no escape. We must set our affections on things above. We must look for joy in that which is rooted and grounded in God's own eternity.

We have scarcely begun to digest this shock before—under the influence of that unfailing habit of self-reference which none but the saints escape from—we begin to calculate our profits and losses. And, fearful of tempting Fate, we prepare for the worst. Does this mean, then, that we have no right to enjoy the next meal, or the next pipe of tobacco? Fortunately for us—this time fortunately for us natural men, moving contentedly between our morning bacon and our evening coffee—it does not. It means what it says. That we must look for joy only in that which comes of God and is willed by God. That we must expect joy only in so far as we accept God's gifts *as* God's gifts, and not as our own private acquisitions. But our

daily meals are certainly the gifts of God. And it is equally
certainly his will that we should eat them. We must not blame
ourselves that God has given us appetites. Nor must we suspect
either God's good intentions or his wisdom in making bacon
pleasing to the palate and coffee soothing to the head. Still less
must we assume that it is the Devil who causes the frying-pan
to give off such a fetching scent. There is no trick in these
allurements: only an honest, open-handed offer, accompanied
by a fair condition. Accept and use these things, my gifts,
remembering that they are my gifts. Use them to the sustaining
and the delighting (that too) of lives spent in obedience.

We take bacon as our example because, however pleasing,
bacon is not romantic. We cannot fabricate a false sentimentality, and substitute it for the truth about the gifts of God, so
long as we deal with things like bacon and coffee. They will
not tolerate it. Of course, when we speak of God's gifts, we
mean greater things too—a mother's love, a baby's innocence,
a young girl's grace—but not only these. Not only the things
that lend themselves to versification on birthday cards and
calendars, but all the things that have rightly pleased you and
me during this very humdrum day. We shall find true joy—
proportionate joy—in them, provided that we receive them as
God's gifts. But receiving them as God's gifts means something
more than remembering to say grace before we start tucking in.
It means ensuring that they are used as he would have them
used. A very tall order, when you come to think about it, even
if applied only to this morning's bacon. For God's demand—
the accompaniment and condition of his gift—is nothing less
than that the body and mind nourished by this morning's
breakfast should in fact operate at his will throughout the
course of the day. Receiving even food as God's gift involves
all that, as well as the duty to eat temperately, always bearing
in mind the need of others first. That again is a seemingly little
point, slipped in by way of qualification. But how widely it

stretches the threads of responsibility stemming from my morning breakfast. That I should eat, having borne in mind the needs of others first; having done something to ensure that they are met.

Oh no, God will not deprive us of our morning bacon: but he will burden its joyful consumption with such a load of responsibilities to our fellow men that perhaps, in sheer self-defence, we shall decide that after all it is easier to do without it. Indeed it is easier. But that is not God's way. He wills that we should accept his gifts, and also that we should accept the massive conditions that accompany them; the call to live in love with all men, answering the needs of our neighbours—including the battered enemy on the highway whom others pass by on the other side.

Thus we cannot defend ourselves either from God's gifts or from his injunctions. We are, in every sense, at the mercy of a giving and commanding God. He showers his gifts upon us from dawn to dusk; food and warmth, shelter and cosiness, sunshine and exercise, agile play of hand and brain. We are drenched in his bounty, soaked to the skin in his free blessings: yet there is not a drop in all that abundance which falls without the uttered word of command. Receive this, and use it wholly and solely as my gift.

And now we may well ask ourselves the question to which all this argument leads. I complain that my specifically religious experience is dry and drab. But is there any life and warmth in me as the daily, hourly recipient of all the manifold blessings of a tirelessly giving God? A God whose infinite inventiveness seems to have been specially exercised in devising abundant and varied delights to gladden the hearts and satisfy the senses of his created children of earth. If I cannot receive and use even my morning breakfast truly and fully as God's gift, am I then ready for the transport of worshipping saints, and the visions of dedicated mystics?

Indeed, indeed we must look for all final surety and repose in that which lies beyond the horizons of our finite world. But we must begin at the beginning. In every sense we are children in the Faith. And we had better first learn to receive our daily food as God's own gift. That is our first lesson. And it is the easiest by far. If we cannot master even that one, there is small hope of our meditating fruitfully on how saints can receive as God's own gift the lash of persecution and the crown of martyrdom.

If I receive the hourly blessings of health, food, vitality, and companionship, without any awareness of their divine origin, then I am certainly not yet in a condition to find through prayer the contemplative's bliss in the divine indwelling, or to catch before the altar a fleeting glimpse of the beatific vision. If you are a wise parent, you will not buy your son an expensive bicycle, when he has shown himself incapable of treating even a scooter with respect. God being our Father, loving and wise, there is no possible evasion of this truth. If we expect to share, through religious observances of worship and sacrament, in the joy of the risen Son, before we have learned to accept life's bread and butter as the bountiful gift of the Father, then we are trying to turn religion and reason upside down.

This, of course, is a question of gratitude. But gratitude is a bigger matter than it is frequently made to appear. There are perhaps too many sermons about saying a verbal "Thank you" to God. Suppose you have two sons, and you give five shillings to each of them. The one son is very profuse in his thanks; but he rushes off to spend the money rashly on sweets and trifles. The other son, less prone to speech, mutters "Thanks" and is then silent. But he goes away and spends the bulk of his money on a bunch of flowers for his mother. There is no doubt where the truer gratitude lies in that example. We are in this situation in relation to God's gifts to us—with a difference. And the difference is that God plainly tells us what he wants us to do with everything he has given us; to use it in his service. There is no true gratitude unless this injunction is obeyed. There is no true gratitude in a whole cycle of verbal thanksgivings to God, if we pocket all his gifts for our private self-indulgence.

That is why we must be wary of "counting our blessings". The phrase is not a happy one. Somehow it reeks of self-interest, seeming to recommend a calculation of profits to date from our commerce with God. The idea of sitting complacently down to a general audit of benefits received and losses incurred, with the intention of satisfying ourselves that we are not in the red over our transactions with the Giver of all things, smacks too much of worldly accountancy. And that is the danger of recommending gratitude to God without explaining what gratitude means. Surely we have all been guilty of false gratitude to God, and perhaps especially after hearing sermons about the one leper who returned to say thank you. To kneel in prayer and to survey in detail all the things in life which have lately brought us pleasure is a smug business indeed, unless every single blessing is considered in relation to the obligations which it imposed and which we have neglected to fulfil.

Since every gift we receive from God comes with a command attached to it, the sum of our argument is this: that gratitude means obedience. But we have already said that joy is obedience, that vocation is obedience, and indeed that the heart of all Christian practice is obedience—self-adjustment to the pattern of things purposed by God. Turn and twist as we may, if we get down earnestly to the question of man's relationship to God, we shall be unable to escape the conclusion that obedience is the beginning and the end of the Christian life. God's will or our will: the great either/or, the issue which dominates our days, sometimes when we least suspect it. It is there, in the background, behind this nagging worry, behind that sudden joy. Perhaps both seem inexplicable at first. They will assume meaning as soon as they are ranged in their proper context, the context of all things that touch us from the cradle to the grave, the context of God's will for us.

But—it must be repeated again—if we cannot put our morning breakfast and our afternoon taste of sunshine into their proper context, how can we expect to keep pace with a great joy—like falling in love, or achieving some long-cherished ambition? If we cannot put a trivial rebuff or an unworthy sneer into its proper context, how can we expect to grapple with a great sorrow—like bereavement or mental depression?

The only true joy is obedience to God. And obedience ranges everything that touches us, joyful or sorrowful, within the pattern of God's good purposes. Thus obedience relates all things that touch us to a source of meaning which is outside time. In this way we set our affections upon things above, expecting joy only in service to God's kingdom. These truths do not by any means recommend us either to turn our backs upon earthly ventures, delights, and solaces, or to escape from hard reality into a continuous mystical day-dream. On the contrary, these truths teach us to see the actualities of earth in their proper perspective, in their true quality, and in their full meaning. To see earthly objects and experiences in their proper *perspective* is to see them as events within a limited finite order whose status is wholly dependent upon a higher, eternal order, and in whose temporal sphere we live but a fleeting, transitory existence. To see earthly objects and experiences in their true *quality* is to see them at all points expressing either value or the denial of value—representing, that is, the impact upon our environment of the assertions of God or the negations of rebellious free will. Lastly, to see earthly objects and experiences in their full *meaning* is to recognize the part they play in God's good purposes for us and, as far as we can, in God's good purposes for all men. It is to relate all good things to him who is their origin and their end; all evil things to him whose good purposes they pervert and betray.

Thus God's great either/or, facing us at every moment of our lives, perhaps only rarely takes the form of the crude alternatives—to have or not to have. Sometimes it does, of course. If I have already eaten enough, then, when my eye catches the iced cake, I am faced with these simple alternatives. But, even over such an apparently simple matter as eating, or over-eating, the issue is frequently not so obvious as that. Have we never felt it our duty to eat an unwanted meal prepared with great delight by some lonely old lady we have visited? Have we never, in good charity, laboriously forced down a piece of her home-made cake, and told her how nice it was, while wishing it a tenth of its size? We are poor Christians if we have never stuffed down unnecessary food in the name of charity.

This example makes a valid point. God's purposes may involve us at one moment in abstaining from food which we want, and at another moment in eating what in fact we neither need nor desire. And if that is not sufficient to show the gaping rift between Christian morality and the ethics of the Stoic or of the healthy-mind-in-a-healthy body psychologist, we can no doubt easily fabricate an even more foolish stumbling-block for the Greeks. But we must not trail the eccentric exceptions. More often than not, the demand of God's will is in accordance with the claims of temperance, health, and sound digestion. Only we must say enough to show that the either/or is rarely a choice between acceptance and self-deprivation in its most obvious form.

So far as the good things of life are concerned, the either/or is more usually a choice between acceptance of the gift only, and acceptance of the gift along with the command that accompanies it. The command is always the same, and it links together the ordinary gift and the more noteworthy gift, the daily meals and the special talent, the blessing of health and the gift of a unique and valued friend. All must be received, and used in God's service. He has purposes for us in relation to all of them. We have got to learn to think in terms of this net of divine conspiracy against our natural selfishness. We have got to learn to say—This is a jolly good breakfast; but I cannot allow a good breakfast to be given to a fellow who is going to waste and squander every ounce of energy and vigour received from it. In receiving this good breakfast, I am, if I keep my part of the bargain, committed by it to God's good purposes for to-day. That was why he gave it to me, the only reason he gave it to me—that I might operate to-day in his service in the way of a healthy, nourished man. If he had wanted me to operate to-day in his service in the way of a sick, suffering man, he could just as easily have given me stomach ulcers, or nausea for everything except bread and milk. And what goes for my breakfast goes for everything I am given; my abounding health, my adequate supply of money, my home and family, my special talents and capacities, my senses and my brain. If we punctiliously thank God daily for these things, and then go off to exploit them all in self-service and self-gratification, in the satisfaction of unredeemed ambition and assertiveness, then we blaspheme in the face of God.

We have said enough in earlier chapters about the acceptance of suffering and failure; and we have now said enough in this chapter about the acceptance of life's good things. In either case, the secret of Christian practice is obedience and self-offering. And in obedience and self-offering alone there is true joy. It follows that, since we have to learn obedience and self-offering, we have therefore to *learn* true joy. This is the logical conclusion of our argument; and it provides the only final answer to the problem of joylessness. Whether we can say that our joy will be proportionate to our obedience is another matter. Differences of environment and of temperament, which are not within our control, will quite plainly have their effect. Nevertheless we have grounds for saying that, if we are troubled by our own lack of joy, whether in our religious experience in particular, or in our daily affairs generally, we have reason to suspect somewhere a failing of obedience. And that failing may well be in what is the least obvious, because the most ordinary place—at the point of our response to the most usual daily gifts of food, sleep, shelter, and the basic means of life.

What we have just said does not, of course, cancel out or in any way invalidate our earlier argument to the effect that our present situation is in many ways peculiarly conducive to gravity. In any situation the practice of obedience will have its own appropriate mode and concomitant temper. Thus the obedience of Christians who are buoyantly conscious of being on good terms with their civilization will not be the same, either in mode or in temper, as the obedience of Christians who are ruefully aware of being at cross-purposes with the dominant movements of contemporary thought. As there are different modes of obedience, so there are different kinds of joy, and we must not look to taste a brand of joy incongruous with the particular kind of obedience required of us by virtue of our historical and personal situation. We should not expect the surgeon, fresh from successfully carrying out a rare and dangerous operation, to express the same kind of joy as, say, the comedian who has just achieved a triumph before a massive audience. This truth does not imply any deficiency in either kind of joy; but surely it makes clear that the joy appropriate to one happy situation is not necessarily appropriate to another. We might expect the surgeon's joy to be disciplined, tight-lipped, grave, and unostentatious. We might expect the comedian's joy to be rollicking, noisy, abandoned, and expansive. Certainly we should think that there was something very odd about a surgeon who rocked with laughter on successfully achieving a triumph of surgery.

However otherworldly our religion may be in its orientation and in its final end, both its theological doctrine and its moral precepts pin us down securely to particular duties in our immediate human environment. We are asked to realize that environment in living and fruitful encounters with our fellow men. Thus, however dry or however ecstatic may be the quality of our individual religious experience, the obedience manifested in our daily work and intercourse with our fellows will take its tone and temper from the quality of that work and intercourse. And in view of what we have said about the spiritual condition of modern civilization—especially urban civilization—it is unlikely that our daily Christian witness will be of a character calculated to keep the temperament vibrant with buoyancy and inspirited with zestful delight. The spiritual tonic merchants, who want to use the Faith, first and foremost, to flood the world with bubbling good-fellowship, are off the mark, out of place, and out of date. They are like evangelistic barrow-boys, peddling ice-cream and hot-dogs in hospital wards where the patients are suffering from acute dyspepsia and only want to be left in peace and quiet with their glasses of milk. There is nothing wicked about this kind of thing: indeed a little of it may be welcome as an entertaining diversion in a drab situation, but as an active expression of earnest ameliorative zeal, it is simply out of gear.

Why is it necessary to say this? Because there are those among us who still think that the appropriate mode of Christian witness to-day is to mingle in any kind of company gently assuring everyone that we are after all only saying what they are saying, but in slightly different words. That at bottom we agree with them all: that in fact our Christian duty is exactly that, to agree with them all, or—as Christ put it—to love them all. That we stand for unlimited tolerance of every view, opinion, and code; that indeed our Christian practice is exactly that, to tolerate every human attitude indiscriminately, or again—as Christ put it—to love everybody. This brand of debased Christianity is so vulnerable to the slightest intellectual attack that one is tempted to imagine that it would be easy to correct it. But in fact, recognizing its own intellectual vulnerability, it eschews intellectual communication of any kind, wrapping itself in a rubber blanket of so-called "charity" which deflects the weapons of logic and reason. This brand of "Christianity" distrusts the rational as being a matter of pure theory, and busies itself in obliterating doctrine and tradition in the name of practical charity.

The adherents of this debased religion gather people together in what is called a spirit of good-fellowship; but it has no basis in agreed rational conviction or in community of faith. The good-fellowship manifested has thus neither more nor less significance than the good-fellowship uniting a body of Moslems or Marxists. The key, pass-word, and symbol of this religion is the indiscriminate smile, which embraces every contact in a bog of undefined comprehensiveness. There have been phases in the history of Christendom (we need only think of the Inquisition) which have made the arm of justice suspect; there have been phases which have made the logical brain suspect; phases which have made ecclesiastical authority suspect; phases which have made monastic withdrawal from the world suspect; others which have made segregation, ritual, or evangelical fervour suspect. But perhaps not until the twentieth century has there been a phase to throw suspicion on the cordial human smile.

The truth is that, in the present situation (which may, of course, change at any time), the need is for Christians to close their ranks, not to open them. The need is for an occasional emotional reticence, a certain social restraint, an inner attitude of withdrawal from the world.

What does withdrawal mean? Certainly not that we must be less active in good works, less ready to help our neighbours, less concerned about the sick and unfortunate, or to any degree less available to those who seek human companionship. But we must be acutely on our guard against social commitments and emotional entanglements with groups of people engaged in communal projects or pleasures, where such commitment and entanglement would imply a community of aim, motive, or inspiration, which in fact does not exist. Whatever our particular vocation—the specific mode of our obedience—may be, it certainly cannot to-day be this: to add further to the general misunderstanding of what the Christian Faith means and what demands it makes upon faithful Christians. It cannot be that we are called to spread further the delusion that everyone who lives cheerfully with his fellows without transgressing the law of the land is a good Christian.

It has been too readily assumed that the Christian Church stands foursquare behind progressive humanistic movements in the spheres of national welfare, culture, education, and social life. There is a sense in which it does. There is also a sense in which it does not. In so far as movements serve the betterment of mankind, physically or mentally, the Christian supports them. In so far as they are exclusively man-centred in their aims, ethos, and motives, the Christian finds them both corrupt and corrupting. That is our dilemma; our tragedy perhaps. Every active support of such movements is falsely interpreted by many as total Christian acquiescence in a humanistic code. Such support is necessary. We must either give it, or retire from life into a cowardly self-centredness. But because our support will be misunderstood, it must be continually counterbalanced by acts of withdrawal calculated to remind our fellow-men that Christianity is not this. Here is a dominating Christian vocation to-day: to move between the assertory and the negatory. This is in many respects good: as such we support it. But it is not Christianity: we cannot be wholly in it to the end.

We enter into such projects; but we enter restrainedly, with reticence, misgivings, reservations. We do not enter with the abounding ebullience of total commitment. Yet because we cannot continually smile, there is no need for a frown. That is why the word *withdrawal* is used here, which carries no emotional overtone, and suggests only a refusal to be fully involved. Withdrawal, fitful or sustained, is not easy. There will be times when we shall be thought, and called, prickly, awkward, uncooperative. There is no need to be afraid of such accusations. Very often they express an uneasy conscience rather than a truly indignant judgement.

To put it all very simply, we live in the midst of many projects objectively worthy of support. Some of us may even be professionally employed in serving them. But, by and large, these projects do not go forward under the impetus of a specifically Christian impulse. They are man-centred, and those who support and forward them, for the most part, leave God out of account. We must serve these projects. Otherwise we cut ourselves off from our own civilization, our own fellow creatures, our human inheritance. Yet we must continually pass judgement upon their limitations. And passing judgement does not mean privately saying, "I don't fully agree with this", while outwardly behaving as though I do. That is treachery and deceit. It means giving open expression to the fundamental divergence of aim which separates the Christian from the pagan, the divergence between living life in the service of God and living it in the service of man.

We are all deeply aware to-day that the life of our Church has been strengthened of late by the increasing number of specialized vocations to the religious life. As we consider the advantages accruing to our common Body, the Church, from this specialized withdrawal, we must also ask ourselves to what extent ordinary laymen and women, whose religious life centres in the parish church, need to exercise in their own daily lives the discipline of withdrawal. It is a most difficult matter to comment upon illustratively. Yet precisely because our Church-manship is misunderstood, and because the line of demarcation between the Church and the world is blurred and rubbed out by secularists and erring Christians, there is pressing need for us to reckon with this "negative" aspect of our Christian vocation. Our regular attendance at worship and our active involvement in Church work need to be supplemented by a picking and choosing in secular commitments which will help to make clear to the world that the Church is the Church. This is no longer merely a matter of private spiritual self-protection, but of public Christian witness; a matter of testifying openly to the Church's status and her claim.

It is almost impossible to exemplify this discipline of withdrawal in concrete terms, because of the infinite diversity of human rôles. But it will be admitted that there are occasions when attendance at certain social gatherings or functions will imply an acquiescence in some ethos or code which the Christian rejects. Perhaps it is a gathering in which we know, from past experience, that conversation will move on a level which presupposes a morality widely divergent from Christian morality—in respect of divorce, for instance. Or perhaps it is a function at which we are quite certain that pronouncements will be made which presuppose equations between humanistic and Christian ideals that are false. It may be the coming together of people whose company and conversation we have long enjoyed, but whose prevailing scepticism has managed always to assimilate and negate our Christian profession by a light, friendly banter which only a prig could openly resent. Worse still, the thing that ought to worry us may be the activities of an organization specifically religious in its basis. It may be that some interdenominational fellowship, which began as a true expression of Christian brotherhood on the part of earnest seekers after truth, has gradually degenerated into an assembly which obliterates denominational differences that are truly important, and fogs doctrine and discipline in a blur of fruitless, mutual self-admiration.

In such instances—and in a hundred others—there is need of the Christian witness of withdrawal. More and more we twentieth-century Christians have got to think, not just in terms of what we actively support, but in terms of what we carelessly and unthinkingly acquiesce in. We are not dealing merely with open evils which provoke our defiance, nor with clearly expressed error that asks for rational contradiction. We are dealing, far too often, with covert evils and subtle implicit errors which invite from us, under cover of charity and good-fellowship, nothing more than the smile and nod of acquiescence. It is a terrible thing to say; but we have to watch our smile. We catch a friendly eye, we hear a friendly accent; and over the coffee cup, the sherry glass, or the committee table, we automatically nod an agreeing nod and, in sheer good will, smile an acquiescent smile. And, in doing so, as we realize a moment later, we have betrayed the Faith in which we were baptized.

Then, having exhausted the resources of our cheerfulness in little acts of betrayal, we begin to complain because our religion does not fill us with the joy of the saints. Indeed it will not. The joy of the saints, in the twentieth century, can never be the buoyant expansiveness of men in league with their own civilization. It will be a joy arising from the peculiar mode of obedience appropriate to our contemporary situation. And that obedience will certainly involve withdrawal; full-scale withdrawal from certain ventures and social gatherings, minor acts of fitful withdrawal from the easy assumptions of those with whom we work and play—the momentary silence replacing the automatic "Yes" of assent; the momentary gravity replacing the automatic smile of acquiescent response; the occasional

"No", and the occasional open protest, when we have so disciplined ourselves that we can combine charity with clarity in our refutations.

Because we are in this situation, our joy—the joy of our growing obedience—will not be a spontaneous, indiscriminate gush, infectiously committing us, heart and soul, to all whom we encounter. It will be a joy learned, like our obedience, through caution and discipline, through gravity and reticence, through costly withdrawals from our world.